In the male who is impotent, his penis fails to respond to erotic stimulation with an erection. The penis remains limp. In the female who is frigid, the vagina remains dry and tight.   Chapter 1

* * *

Diabetes can bring with it sexual difficulties and arousal failure. Prostate problems in men can bring an end to sexual intercourse.

Chapter 3

* * *

Where husband and wife are both obese, the abdominal girth may be so large that intravaginal coitus is impossible.   Chapter 5

* * *

Following a mastectomy, sexual behavior in the female may change. The frequency of sexual intercourse may decrease.

Chapter 6

* * *

A hysterectomy may change sexual patterns. The wife may become a nymphomaniac. Nymphomania is an abnormally excessive sexual desire by the female.   Chapter 7

* * *

Many prescription drugs including diuretics and drugs given for high blood pressure can reduce the sex drive considerably.

Chapter 8

* * *

Alcohol, cigarettes and addictive drugs like marijuana, cocaine, heroin and amphetamines . . . all **reduce** the sex drive!   Chapter 10

* * *

In the battle of the bedroom . . . for subtle revenge . . . the wife may exercise power dominance during initial lovemaking in order to make her husband incapable of performing sexually.   Chapter 14

* * *

The wife may want clitoral stimulation so she can have an orgasm. The man may think the missionary position is the only proper way for orgasm. Continued frustration by husband or wife in not having sexual desires met can lead to impotence and frigidity.   Chapter 15

* * *

All this and much more you will find in the chapters of this revealing book that shows **How To Win Over Impotence/Frigidity!**

HOW
TO WIN
OVER
IMPOTENCE/FRIGIDITY

by Salem Kirban

Library of Congress Catalog Card No. 81-83271
ISBN 0-912582-42-1

ACKNOWLEDGMENTS

To **Estelle Bair Composition** for excellent craftsmanship in setting the type.

To **Walter W. Slotilock,** Chapel Hill Litho, for negatives.

To **Koechel Designs,** for an excellent cover design.

To **Bob Jackson,** for medical illustrations on pages 82, 110, 114.

To **Dickinson Brothers, Inc.,** for printing this book.

And special thanks to the following publishers for graciously making available medical illustrations for this book:

Intermed Communications, Inc., Horsham, Pennsylvania 19004
Illustrations reprinted with permission from <u>Diseases,</u> Copyright ©1981.

J.B. Lippincott Company, Philadelphia, Pennsylvania 19105
Illustrations reprinted with permission from <u>Textbook of Medical-Surgical Nursing</u> by L. Brunner and D. Suddarth, ed. 4, Copyright ©1980.

Mitchell Beazley Publishers, Ltd., England
<u>Atlas of the Body and Mind,</u> Copyright ©Mitchell Beazley Publishers, Ltd. 1976. Published in U.S.A. by **Rand McNally & Company.**

Sally Galbraith Thomas, R.N., Ph.D., Associate Professor, School of Nursing, University of California, Los Angeles, California 90024, for permission to use photograph on breast cancer on page 32.

CONTENTS

Special Features Include

WHY I WROTE THIS BOOK

In the last 12 years I have written over 45 books. All my books are written to uplift people's lives ... emotionally, physically ... and most of all, spiritually.

As a writer, I have a responsibility to be honest to my calling. Sometimes I write books because there is a real _need_ for a subject to be covered. Although I realize that the very writing of them will bring criticism in some circles.

It would be much easier for me to write books that the general public _wants_. And such writing would rapidly increase my income.

However, as an author, I feel compelled to write books
not based on the public **wants**
but rather, on the public **needs**.

HOW TO WIN OVER IMPOTENCE/FRIGIDITY is such a book.

A rare few would ever admit to a friend (or indeed to their husband, wife or even their doctor) that they are impotent or experience frigidity.

Yet, because of our fast-paced way of life ... the problems of impotence and frigidity are rapidly increasing. No longer is it simply a problem of married couples in their 50's and 60's ... it is now a common problem even among young married couples in their teens and twenties!

Much damage is continually done by popular centerfold sex-oriented magazines. They have warped the beauty of the God-created sexual union of husband with wife. They have taken love and turned it to lust. This misrepresentation of sexual intercourse is to blame for much of the impotence/frigidity problems people face today!

It is my hope that this book will remove both the mystery and the misinformation about sex. And in so doing, it is also my hope that such knowledge will help restore the vibrancy of marriage ... bringing a lasting flame of devotion, happiness and joy.

That's why I wrote this book.

Salem Kirban

Huntingdon Valley, Pennsylvania
U.S.A. September, 1981

1

WHEN SEXUAL UNION FAILS

What Is Impotence/ Frigidity?

Some time in life a man will experience an episode of impotence and a woman may have a period in which she is frigid.

Just what is impotence and frigidity, by definition?

Impotence is not considered an accurate term for the sexual problems many men face. The more accurate description would be *erectile dysfunction*. However, for the sake of brevity, we will call it . . . impotence.

Impotence is defined as:

> . . . the inability of the man
> to perform the sexual act
> because of failure
> to achieve or to sustain
> an erection
> sufficient to complete intercourse.

Frigidity is loosely defined as:

> . . . a coldness and indifference
> to the sexual act
> which results in an inability
> to respond to sexual intercourse
> and to experience sexual pleasure.

A more accurate description of frigidity would be *female sexual dysfunction*.

Inability To Achieve Erection

Impotence in the male, in a sense, is similar to the problem of frigidity in the female.

In the male who is impotent, his penis fails to respond to erotic stimulation with an erection. The penis remains limp (*flaccid*). While it rarely happens, the male can ejaculate with a limp penis.

A Dry Vagina

In the female who is frigid, the vagina remains dry and tight. Yet the unresponsive female can climax even though she has not lubricated.

3 Reasons

Helen Singer Kaplan, M.D., Ph.D., in her book, The New Sex Therapy, suggests both the male and the female with sexual problems generally fall into three categories of sexual dysfunction.[1]

In the Male
1. Impotence
2. Retarded ejaculation
3. Premature ejaculation

In the Female
1. Frigidity
2. Vaginismus
3. Orgastic dysfunction

Understanding the functional problems is the first step towards the solution.

IMPOTENCE

Sexual Conflict

Dr. Kaplan suggests that all three male sexual dysfunctions have a basic underlying cause and appear to be associated with

[1] Helen Singer Kaplan, M.D., Ph.D., The New Sex Therapy (New York: Times Books) 1974, p. 250.

some kind of <u>sexual conflict.</u>

**3
Areas
Of
Conflict**

It can be:

1. <u>Intrapsychic</u>
   An emotional inbalance that
   exists within the mind.

2. <u>Marital</u>
   A conflict in marriage with your
   partner.

3. <u>Guilt</u>
   A conflict borne from some
   emotional experience that links
   intercourse with a fear or a guilt.

Impotence has nothing to do with sterility. And the overwhelming cause of impotence appears to be psychosomatic.

**A Problem
Of Mind
And body**

<u>Psychosomatic</u> is a combination of two words which mean <u>mind</u> and <u>body</u>. Those in the health field recognize the importance of mind-body interrelationship in all illnesses. And, quite often, the subconscious mind, can generate the problem of impotence.

Primary and Secondary Impotence

There are two types of impotence:

**A
Chronic
Condition**

1. <u>Primary impotence</u>
   The male with primary impotence has never been able to have sexual intercourse. He may attain good erections by masturbating or in other situations but he is unable to function with a woman.

   Primary impotence is a chronic condition but it is far less prevalent than secondary impotence.

**A
Passing
Condition**

2. Secondary impotence

The male with secondary impotence has succeeded in completing sexual intercourse in the past but suffers from temporary or fleeting times when he is unable to complete the sexual act. This is a common form of impotence experienced by over half the adult male population.

It has been reported that Carlos II, King of Spain (1665 to 1700), probably suffered from primary impotence. He was unable to father a child to perpetuate the monarchy. This led to the war of the Spanish Succession.

SEX AND PHYSICAL ILLNESS

**10
Organic
Causes**

Impotence may be due to an organic reason. Some 10-15% of men affected by impotence appear to have a physical impairment.

In the Textbook of Sexual Medicine, 10 organic causes are outlined. They include:

1. Anatomic Causes such as hydrocele *(accumulation of fluid in the testicles),* or testicular fibrosis *(abnormal formation of fibrous tissue in testicles).*
2. Cardiorespiratory Causes
3. Drug Ingestion including alcohol, addictive drugs and drugs prescribed medically.
4. Endocrine Causes such as Cushing's syndrome, Diabetes, and Addison's disease.
5. Genitourinary Causes
6. Hematologic Causes such as Hodgkin's disease, Leukemia and Sickle cell anemia.
7. Infectious Causes such as Gonorrhea and mumps.
8. Neurologic Causes such as Cerebral palsy, Multiple sclerosis and Parkinson's disease.
9. Vascular Causes
10. Miscellaneous Causes such as kidney failure, cirrhosis, obesity and herbicide poisoning.[1]

---

[1] Robert C. Kolodny, M.D., William H. Masters, M.D., Virginia E. Johnson, D.Sc. (Hon.), Textbook of Sexual Medicine (Boston: Little, Brown and Company) 1979, pp. 508, 509.

New Light On Impotence

In the past much of medical thinking concluded that the vast majority of men suffering from impotence have underlying emotional problems as the cause of their inability to engage consistently in sexual intercourse.

They arrived at this conclusion because they believed that any evidence of the physical ability to have an erection—such as early morning erections—indicates that the machinery is intact and the cause of impotence is not physical.[1]

However, the Journal of the American Medical Association (February 22/29, 1980) included a report by researchers from the Beth Israel Hospital which reflects new light on impotence.

ENDOCRINE DISORDERS

The Sex Hormone

They tested 105 men who had the problem of impotence. Of this 105, 37 (or 35%) turned out to have unsuspected endocrine disorders.[2] Screening tests turned up ab-

---

[1]G. Timothy Johnson, M.D., Stephen E. Goldfinger, M.D., Harvard Medical School Health Letter Book (Cambridge, Massachusetts: Harvard University Press) 1981, p. 204.

[2]Endocrine system regulates and integrates the body's metabolic activities. The endocrine glands include the pituitary, the thyroid, the parathyroid, adrenal, islands of Langerhans of the pancreas and the gonads (ovaries and testes). Dysfunction can occur when an inadequate amount of the hormone (or hormones) is secreted or if an excessive amount is secreted.

normal levels of the male hormone *testosterone*. With proper therapy, 33 of the 37 experienced restoration of their potency.

Testosterone accelerates growth in tissues and stimulates blood flow. It is essential for normal sexual behaviour and the occurrence of erections.

It is also essential for normal growth and development of the male accessory sexual organs. It also affects many metabolic activities.

Proper Balance Needed

The measured production of testosterone is controlled by a complex triangle hormonal system: the hypothalamus, the pituitary and the gonadal glands. (The gonadal glands are the sex glands.) By seeking to achieve a proper balance, where there is an endocrine imbalance, potency can be renewed.

DIABETIC IMPOTENCE

Sexual Potency Affected

Diabetic Impotence is a disease of the nervous system. However, both men and women experience sexual dysfunction.

In diabetic impotence, the impulse that stimulates the penile arteries to dilate is impeded, hindering engorgement of blood vessels necessary for an erection.

Loss Of Erection Capacities

Erection results when blood collects in and distends the penis. The dilation of the arteries is under nervous control. In some diabetics there is an inability of the nerve impulses to dilate the arteries of the penis

Sexual Myths

Is masturbation dangerous to your physical or mental health?
No! Masturbation, in fact, can give physical release from pent-up anxieties. Children brought up in a restrictive religious atmosphere are often taught that masturbation is a sin. Two Bible passages usually quoted (Genesis 38:8-11 and 1 Corinthians 6:9,10) are lifted out of context and do not refer to masturbation.

Herbert J. Miles teaches Marriage and Family classes in a church-related college. After seminary, he was a pastor for 20 years in Baptist churches. In his book, Sexual Understanding Before Marriage, he writes that because of the male sex drive, a man:

> ... may practice, without being sinful, a limited, temporary program of masturbation from the time he approaches a peak in his sexual drive until he is married.[1]

Dr. J. Jones Stewart, a specialist in sex therapy with a Southern Baptist background states that masturbation is *not* a sin. With over 40 years of medical practice, Dr. Stewart counsels with many couples raised in a Bible-based home. He advises them that masturbation before marriage is a natural outlet for men and women to relieve themselves. (See page 64 for other advice by Dr. Stewart)

Other church groups, however, disagree with the above believing that masturbation is a sin and should not be practiced. Studies show that less than 7% of parents ever talk to their children about masturbation.

The sex organ can never be overused. Masturbation does not cause blindness nor will you wear out your sex organ.[2]

Does penis size have anything to do with making sex better?
Penis size has nothing to do with good sex. The vagina can expand or contract to accommodate any size penis.[3]

Should intercourse be limited to only when a child is desired?
No! Husband and wife should engage regularly in sexual intercourse not just for procreation but for satisfying pleasure and joy.

Should you lose interest in sex as you get older?
No! Physiologically, our body functions slow down with age. But after childbearing years women often become more sexually active. An active sex life even in your 70's and 80's can help prolong your life. If your marriage partner is no longer living, masturbation can relieve the sexual tension and give you a healthy release.

---

[1]Herbert J. Miles, Sexual Understanding Before Marriage (Grand Rapids, Michigan: Zondervan Publishing House) 1971, p. 147.
[2]Andra J. Allen, All American Sexual Myths (New York: American Journal of Nursing) October, 1975, p. 1771.
[3]Ibid., p. 1771.

and to maintain engorgement of the organ with blood.

**Unable
To Maintain
An
Erection**

The individual may experience nocturnal emissions and morning erections caused without any erotic stimuli. The man's sex drive may be strong as ever . . . but he finds himself unable to maintain an erection. Such a condition needs an understanding wife.

The impotence is irreversible; administration of testosterone brings no benefit. Masturbation also fails to achieve an erection.

Some diabetic men achieve orgasm, but incompetence of the bladder neck allows the seminal fluid to flow back into the bladder (retrograde ejaculation) instead of being propelled outward.

No drastic therapeutic measures for impotence are recommended as long as the patient responds to some stimulation. As a last resort, however, a mechanical device — such as Flexirod (two semirigid silastic rods) or Scott-Hydraulic (inflatable tubes) — may be implanted surgically to obtain an erection.

Diabetic women also have orgasmic difficulties. They develop gradually some 6 months to a year after the onset of diabetes.[1]

---

[1]John Blandy, Operative Urology (London: Blackwell Scientific Publications) 1978, pp. 186, 187.

For complete insight into Diabetes, you may wish to order DIABETES *by Salem Kirban. Send $6 (includes postage) to: Salem Kirban, Inc., Kent Rd., Huntingdon Valley, Pa. 19006.*

How Illness Can Affect
The MALE Sexually

Disorder	Possible Sexual Problem
Heart disease Arthritis Cancer Kidney disease	May decrease sexual desire and lengthen time needed to achieve erection. May also affect ability to maintain an erection.

Diseases of the Liver:
  Cirrhosis
  Hepatitis
  Mononucleosis
	May reduce sex drive because of build-up of estrogen levels due to malfunctioning liver.

Endocrine disorders:
  Addison's disease
  Cushing's disease
  Hypogonadism
  Hypopituitarism
  Diabetes
	May decrease sexual desire and impair erection. May bring about impotence.

Genital diseases:
  Herpes simplex
  Chordee[1]
  Peyronie's disease[2]
  Phimosis[3]
  Prostatitis
	May decrease sexual desire and even cause impotence. Because of damage to the genital organs, intercourse may become painful.

Vascular diseases:
  Thrombosis of veins
  or arteries of penis
  Leukemia
  Sickle cell disorders
	Erection may be impaired because of interference with blood supply. Ejaculation and sexual desires will remain intact.

---

[1]Chordee is the downward, painful curvature of the penis on erection in gonorrhea caused by inflammation of the spongy muscle tissue.

[2]Peyronie's disease is the hardening of the spongy muscle tissue which distorts the erection of the penis.

[3]Phimosis is a narrowing of the preputial orifice so that the foreskin cannot be pushed back over the glans penis. This is corrected by circumcision.

How Illness Can Affect
The FEMALE Sexually

Disorder	Possible Sexual Problem
Heart disease Arthritis Cancer Kidney disease	May decrease sexual desire. Because of possible pain and depression sexual arousal may be impaired.

Disease of the Liver:
  Cirrhosis
  Hepatitis
  Mononucleosis
	Increased fatigue and irregular estrogen output may reduce sex drive.

Endocrine disorders:
  Addison's disease
  Cushing's disease
  Hypothyroidism
  Hypopituitarism
  Diabetes
	May decrease sexual desire and reduce ability for sexual arousal.

Genital disorders:
  Infection
  Imperforate hymen[1]
  Hymenal tags
  Vulvitis
  Leukoplakia[2]
  Bartholin cyst infection[3]
  Hemorrhoids
  Tight clitoral hood[4]
  Poor episiotomy
	May decrease sexual desire and even cause loss of orgasm. Sexual arousal may be impaired. Chronic condition can bring frigidity.

---

[1] Imperforate hymen is when the covering over the vagina has no opening thus blocking menstrual flow. Hymenal tags are flaps of hymen skin left after hymen has been perforated. They sometimes can become irritated and inflamed.

[2] Leukoplakia is a formation of smooth, irregular, hard white spots or patches on the mucous membrane of the vulva. They may become malignant.

[3] Bartholin Cyst infection is an infection of the Bartholin glands which are situated in the vagina below the vestibule, one on each side of the vaginal opening. They disperse lubricant fluid during intercourse.

[4] Clitoral hood is the skin which covers the small knob of tissue called the clitoris. The clitoris in the female is similar in its sensitivity and erection to the penis in the male. If the clitoral hood is tight, it will interfere with the clitoral erection and interfere with the ability of the clitoris to be equisitely stimulated for orgasm.

3

DISEASES OF THE PENIS AND PROSTATE

**A
Curved
Penis**

Peyronie's disease of the penis is an uncommon but sexually handicapping problem. It occurs most often in men between
ages 40 and 60.

Scar tissue on the penis makes the penis
curve when it is in the erection stage. Men
with Peyronie's disease may experience
pain when an erection occurs. This pain
could discourage intercourse and cause
impotency. In some cases this is corrected
surgically by removing the plaque of fibrous tissue and making a skin graft to
eliminate the curving tendency. Surgeons
are hesitant to perform this surgery because the patient may still be impotent
after surgery. Refashioning his penis may
prevent deformity but may not cure the impotence.[1]

---

[1]John Blandy, Operative Urology (London: Blackwell
Scientific Publications) 1978, pp. 186, 187.

A Continual Erection

Priapism is *a persistent state of penis erection that is usually independent of sexual arousal.* The most common causes are sickle cell anemia, leukemia and polycythemia *(an excess of red blood cells).* Priapism is an abnormal, painful and continued erection, usually without sexual desire. It requires immediate surgery. Delayed treatment will cause permanent damage making it impossible to have sexual erections thus resulting in impotency.

PROSTATE ILLS THAT CAN OCCUR

Things Go Wrong!

As men grow older, instead of performing heroic functions, the prostate tends to become the General of Malfunctions! Let's look at some problems that can occur.

1. Prostatitis (Acute and Chronic)
2. Prostatism (Enlarged Prostate)
3. Cancer of the Prostate

PROSTATITIS (ACUTE)

A Bacterial Injection

Acute Prostatitis is a common ailment that affects men from young adulthood on. It is a bacterial infection of the prostate gland.

The symptoms may develop slowly but acute prostatitis is characterized by the rather abrupt onset of fever. There is also pain at the base of the penis and painful urination. There may be uncontrolled dripping of cloudy fluid from the urethra

The Prostate And Sex

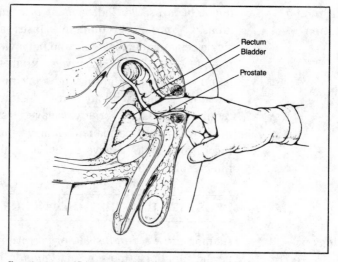

Illustration courtesy J.B. Lippincott Company: Brunner, L., Suddarth, D.: Textbook of Medical-Surgical Nursing. ed. 4, 1980, Philadelphia, J.B. Lippincott.

About 35% of men over age 50 have <u>chronic prostatitis</u>. Low back pain, frequent and urgent urination and painful ejaculation are some of the indicators of this problem. <u>Prostate cancer</u> is the second most common cancer found in men over age 50. Unexplained cystitis, difficulty in starting urinary stream, dribbling, urine retention are possible indicators of prostate cancer. The rectal examination is an essential part of a physical check-up for all men over 40.

BENIGN PROSTATIC HYPERPLASIA

NORMAL PROSTATE

ENLARGED PROSTATE

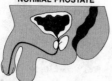

As the prostate gland expands, it compresses the urethra and bladder, obstructing urinary flow.

through the penis. One might feel an incomplete emptying of the bladder. Chills and fever are also a clue.

It frequently occurs in young men from 20 to 35. It can be a problem associated with some venereal diseases as well.

PROSTATIS (CHRONIC)

**A
Nagging
Problem**

Chronic prostatitis can be a more difficult problem because, often, no bacteria can be identified as the certain cause. In chronic prostatitis there is usually no fever but a great frequency of urination. There is loss of libido *(desire for sexual intercourse)*. There may also be times when the man is impotent *(inability to ejaculate sperm)*.

Some doctors believe that emotions can play a part in chronic prostatitis.

> Caffeine-containing beverages, decreased sexual activity, prolonged sitting, and many other factors have been associated in popular myth with prostate infections, but scientific evidence does not support these as significant causes.[1]

PROSTATISM
(Benign Prostatic Hypertrophy)

**The
Enlarged
Prostate**

Hypertrophy means *an increase in the size of an organ which does not involve tumor formation.* Thus, in prostatism, the prostate is enlarged. Because the symptoms are

[1]G. Timothy Johnson, M.D. and Stephen E. Goldfinger, M.D., Health Letter Book (Cambridge, Mass.: Harvard University Press) 1981, p. 382.

somewhat similar, it is often confused with prostatitis.

Urination During Sleeping Hours A Clue

However, prostatism is a gradual noninfectious, noncancerous enlargement of the prostate gland. The problem may not evidence itself for many years and when the symptoms start, they may be almost unnoticeable. There may be a tendency to drain a little urine after urination seems complete. One may experience *nocturia*, the necessity to urinate two or three times or more at night.

Symptoms include:

> Pain the prostate region
> Discomfort on sitting
> Urgent, painful, burning urination
> Stream of urine that is feeble
>   and dribbles
> Pain during ejaculation at intercourse
> Unexplained bouts of impotence
> Premature ejaculation
> Low back pain

When the prostate increases in size, it can disturb the function of the urethra. Because the prostate gland surrounds the urethra ... one can see, as it enlarges, it would narrow the passageway for the urine to flow.

Too Much Sex Stimulation

There are some that believe that prostatism (enlarged prostate) often has its roots in youth. This is the time when sex stimulation is high and relief is low.

> Petting, for example,
> overextends sexual tension
>   without normal release

within a reasonable time,
thus keeping the prostate
  in an overworked state
  for too long and too often.

Continence *(self-restraint)*
may be even more injurious to the
    prostate.
The manufactured sperm is retained
    with no place to go,
    putting an additional burden
    on that gland.

This concept
has not been fully accepted
by the medical profession.[1]

For some reason not precisely known, the prostate begins to enlarge at about age 40. About two out of every three men over 60 have some degree of prostatic enlargement. Enlargement may be caused by some hormone relationship.

CANCER OF THE PROSTATE

Rectal Examination Important

Cancer of the prostate is one of the major causes of cancer deaths in men ... about 20,000 per year in the United States. Doctors recommend annual rectal examinations in males over age 50 so that this disease can be detected in its early stages. Most prostate cancers occur in the rear part of the prostate gland. And this can easily be felt during a rectal examination.

The glandular tissue of the prostate resembles that of a woman's breast. Some

[1]Sigmund S. Miller, Symptoms (New York: Avon Books) 1978, p. 428.

believe that the cancers are similar. The symptoms of cancer of the prostate are somewhat similar to those of an enlarged prostate. It is identified by the doctor because of the hard, irregular lumps that can be felt during a rectal exam.

If not treated, the disease can spread to other areas of the body such as the bone of the pelvis or the spine. A rise in the level of the enzyme *acid phosphatase* in the serum may indicate cancer of the prostate.

Ejaculation Force Lessened

In cancer of the prostate where a total prostatectomy is performed, impotence is almost always to be expected. If the patient does not want to give up sexual activity, a plastic insert may be used to make the penis rigid for sexual intercourse.

There is a theory that sexual activity may help to prevent prostate cancer. It is believed that sex hormones build up during abstinence and possibly reduce the prostate cells' immunity significantly.[1]

After any prostate surgery . . . if sexual intercourse is possible, the force of the ejaculation will be lessened.

---

[1]Medical Aspects of Human Sexuality/a monthly magazine published in New York.

For complete information on the Prostate, you may wish to order PROSTATE PROBLEMS by Salem Kirban. Send $6 (includes postage) to: Salem Kirban, Inc., Kent Road, Huntingdon Valley, Pa. 19006.

4

HOW CHRONIC ILLNESS AFFECTS SEX

**Underlying
Causes**

Chronic illnesses can also have an effect on one's sexual performance.

Multiple Sclerosis

Multiple Sclerosis affects the transmission of impulses through the central nervous system causing impotence of impairment of female orgasm.[1]

In a questionnaire sent to 302 men and women with multiple sclerosis, 64% of the men and 39% of the women reported having an unsatisfactory sex life or having stopped participation in sexual activity. About 80% of the men had difficulty with erection and 57% of the women had difficulty achieving orgasm. Because of multiple sclerosis fluctuating condition, there are times when sexual performance can be very satisfactory. Continued sexual activity is essential to overcome the problem.[2]

---

[1]*Orgasm is a state of joyous emotional excitement that occurs at the climax of sexual intercourse. In the male it is accompanied by ejaculation of semen. In the female it is accompanied by pulsating uncontrollable movements mostly in the pelvic area.*

[2]Robert C. Kolodny, M.D., William H. Masters, M.D., Virginia E. Johnson, D.Sc. (Hon), Textbook of Sexual Medicine (Boston: Little, Brown and Company) 1979, pp. 258, 259.

Lung Diseases

Lung diseases such as emphysema encourage impotence because sexual excitement requires increased oxygen demands.

A Possible Solution

In some studies made of men suffering from either emphysema or chronic bronchitis, 39% of the men reported total impotence for one or more years. In some cases there was impaired sensory and motor nerves which made the mechanics of erection difficult. Therapy included suggesting the use of a waterbed. This lessened the degree of physical activity of those with breathing problems. Then, too, the active movement of the healthy partner produces a fluid wave which automatically propels the inactive person ... according to the authors of Textbook of Sexual Medicine.

Arthritis

Chronic arthritis may cause impotence or frigidity because the positions of sexual intercourse cause arthritic pain. This is often helped by the male and female adopting other intercourse positions than those normally used.

For complete information on Arthritis, you may wish to order ARTHRITIS *by Salem Kirban, Send $6 (includes postage) to: Salem Kirban, Inc., Kent Road, Huntingdon Valley, Pa. 19006.*

Strokes

**Decreases
Desire**

In a study made of 105 stroke patients less than 60 years old, some 60% did not experience a loss of sexual desire (libido). It was discovered that sexual desire decreased if the right side was paralyzed . . . more so than in left-side paralysis.

Generally the mechanical difficulties and the emotional factors encourge impotence and frigidity.

Systematic Lupus Erythematosus

**Sexual
Function
Varies**

This is a chronic disease of unknown origin. It affects women more frequently than men (9:1) and occurs usually during the reproductive years. Sexual function varies.

Skin changes occur as can arthritis. Ulcers in the mouth and vagina may create pain upon sexual contact. Because this is treated with cortisone, drug-related sexual difficulties can occur because of increase in vaginal infections and ceasing of menstrual flow (amenorrhea).

5

HOW OBESITY CAUSES SEX PROBLEMS

Poor Accessibility

Obesity may encourage both impotence in the male and frigidity in the female. The simple mechanics of reaching the genital area may be difficult because of poor accessibility.

In our society, overweight (obese) persons are generally thought of, unfortunately, as unattractive and unable to control impulsive behavior. Obesity can be considered a chronic illness. There are some who are physically attracted to an obese person, but this is the exception, not the rule.

Low Sex Hormone

In a study of 22 obese males, tests showed that they had a lower level of the sex hormone, testosterone. The more overweight they were, the lower the hormone level. All of the patients had normal size testicles and normal patterns of masculation. Only two complained that they had a low sex drive. In this research none of the 22 experienced impotence.[1]

---

[1]Robert C. Kolodny, M.D., William H. Masters, M.D., Virginia E. Johnson, D.Sc. (Hon.), Textbook of Sexual Medicine (Boston: Little, Brown and Company) 1979, p. 250.

Obese women have a higher rate of menstrual dysfunction than women of normal weight. Diabetes is associated with a high rate of sexual problems and many obese persons are diabetic.

Low Self-Esteem Impairs Sexual Function

Obesity can bring about psychological problems that can affect sexual performance. Many obese persons have problems with their body-image and self-esteem. In many instances an obese person may marry at the first opportunity in an attempt to upgrade their self-esteem . . . even when the available partner is not really suitable for them.

In the Textbook of Sexual Medicine it is pointed out that there may be mechanical difficulties with sexual intercourse. These problems relate to the proper positioning for coitus.[1]

Coitus May Be Impossible

In the case of two severely obese persons, the abdominal girth may be so large that intravaginal coitus is impossible. This can encourage impotence in the male and frigidity in the female.

Because of excessive weights of the partners, the normal sexual positions where the male or female is underneath the other partner generates a very uncomfortable position and discourages sex.

---

[1]Coitus is the act of sexual intercourse between a man and woman. It is the insertion of the penis into the vagina during sexual arousal, followed by movements of the bodies of both partners that bring about increasing sexual excitement until a climax, or orgasm, is reached.

3

Alternatives

The authors of the Textbook of Sexual Medicine suggest alternatives where both husband and wife are obese that may correct sexual dysfunctions.

These alternatives include:

1. Oral-genital sex
2. Manual stimulation of the genitals
3. Intramammary coitus[1]

In an interesting study, when both husband and wife were obese, each had a protective and stabilizing effect on the other. When one subsequently lost weight, there was a higher incidence of sexual and marital problems for both spouses.[2]

---

[1]When both husband and wife are obese, vaginal intercourse (coitus) may be difficult. Intramammary coitus is an option. In this form of coitus, the husband's penis is placed between the breasts for thrusting stimulation.

[2]Ibid., p. 252.

6

HOW CANCER AFFECTS SEX

Doctors
Fail
To Advise

Often it is *"convenient"* for the physician to *"forget"* that the person with cancer continues to have real sexual needs and fulfillment. Most physicians have done little research in this field and tend to shy away from a brief counselling session on sexual therapy.

The orthodox medical treatment for cancer can in itself be devastating to the individual and quickly diminish his or her sexual desires. Impotence in the male and frigidity in the female can occur overnight.

The loss of hair (*alopecia*) and the loss of appetite (*anorexia*), the nausea and vomiting during chemotherapy treatments can quickly discourage sexual intercourse.

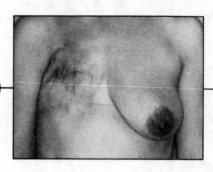

REVEALING INSIGHT

R. R. Grinker reveals some
insight into the problem one
faces with cancer:

The dread of exposing oneself
to one's spouse as
crippled, damaged, incomplete or dying
may cause
sexual inhibition or abstinence

Intimacy and sexual bodily functions
may be affected
by shame and embarrassment

Mutilation *(mastectomy)*
may make exposure and nudity
extremely painful.

There may be
an increase
in the need for contact
and reassurance . . .

On the other hand,
there may be outrage
that the partner displays
any interest in sex.[1]

[1] R. R. Grinker, Sex and Cancer (Medical Aspects of Human Sexuality) 1976, 10(2): 130-139.

Photograph courtesy of Sally Galbraith Thomas, R.N., Ph.D., School of Nursing, University of California.

4
Fears
Women
Face

Mastectomy

Mastectomy is the removal of one or both breasts surgically. Almost 100,000 new cases of breast cancer occur each year. Breast cancer accounts for the highest incidence of female cancer (26%). There is a 65% 5-year survival rate.

When a woman is first told she has breast cancer, her first concern is survival. She may also have many other conflicting emotions which include:

1. Fear of mutilation
2. Anxiety about rejection by husband
3. Fear of insecurity
4. Fear how others will respond

M.H. Witkin suggests that in women with breast cancer:

> The pain of rejection
> increases with intimacy,
> and the woman's greatest fears
> revolve around the man with whom
> she is most intimate.
>
> What many women fear
> is not only rejection
>   in the form of aversion or denial
> but also rejection
>   in the form of pity . . .
>
> Pity implies a belief
> that the woman has really diminished,
> and involves
> not a sharing of her feelings
> but a reinforcement of her fantasies
> of incompleteness and worthlessness.[1]

[1]M. H. Witkin, Sex Therapy and Mastectomy (Journal of Sex and Marital Therapy) 1975, 1:290-304.

NODAL INVOLVEMENT IN CANCER OF THE VULVA

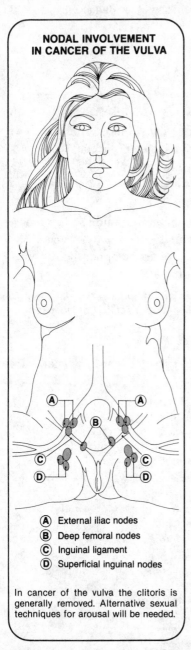

(A) External iliac nodes
(B) Deep femoral nodes
(C) Inguinal ligament
(D) Superficial inguinal nodes

In cancer of the vulva the clitoris is generally removed. Alternative sexual techniques for arousal will be needed.

TYPES OF HYSTERECTOMY

There are three types of hysterectomy: subtotal hysterectomy, total hysterectomy, and total hysterectomy with a salpingo-oophorectomy. The excised portion (which is shaded) varies in each one. In each of these procedures, however, the external genitalia and the vagina are left intact, and the woman is able to resume sexual relations.

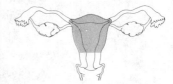

In a *subtotal hysterectomy*, all but the distal portion of the uterus is removed. The cervix is left in place. If the woman is not menopausal, she will continue to menstruate.

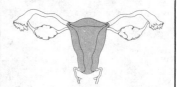

In a *total hysterectomy*, the entire uterus and the cervix are removed. This woman will no longer menstruate.

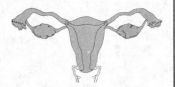

In a *total hysterectomy with a salpingo-oophorectomy*, the uterus, the cervix, the fallopian tubes, and the ovaries are removed. This woman will no longer menstruate.

Sexual Behavior Changes

In the 3-month period immediately after surgery women who had mastectomies had numerous changes in their sexual behavior . . . according to a pilot study made by Masters & Johnson Institute.

There were 49% who resumed intercourse within one month of hospital discharge. But about 33% did not resume intercourse for as long as 6 months after hospitalization.

Coital orgasm[1] experiences changed as well.

> The percentage of women
>   experiencing orgasm
>   during half or more of
>   coital opportunities
>   decreased following mastectomy
>   from 61% to 45%.

> The frequency of women
>   never or rarely
>   having coital orgasm
>   rose from 17% prior to mastectomy
>   to 40% in the first 3 months
>   after mastectomy.[2]

Frequency Of Intercourse Diminishes

The frequency of intercourse also decreased for women after mastectomy. And women who initiated intercourse prior to their mastectomy generally preferred to wait for their husband to initiate the act. If

---

[1]Coital orgasm *is the pulsating climax of excitement that comes from sexual intercourse.*

[2]Robert E. Kolodny, M.D., William H. Masters, M.D., Virginia E. Johnson, D.Sc. (Hon.), Textbook of Sexual Medicine (Boston: Little, Brown and Company) 1979, p. 278.

there is lack of communication in these matters between husband and wife ... these changes could lead to an impotent/frigid relationship.

Sexual Approaches Change

The report also showed a decrease in breast stimulation by the husband on the remaining breast of the wife.

The position of intercourse changed in many of the women who had mastectomy. They preferred the female-superior position for sexual intercourse.

7

SEX AND EMOTIONAL ILLNESS

Emotions
Affect
Sex

It is not every day that one is emotionally sitting on top of a mountain. For every mountain, there is a valley. And emotions vary from day to day, from circumstance to circumstance. These emotions, in today's frantic lifestyle, are perhaps greater accentuated or marked than in the lifestyle of 25 or 30 years ago.

Depression

A Major
Health Problem

Depression is a mental state marked by negative mood changes. These can include:

1. Sadness
2. Loneliness
3. Apathy, lack of interest
4. Persistent feelings
   of low self-esteem
   and self-blame

Depression is a major health problem in the United States. It can be brought about by marital problems, illness, divorce, job loss, conflicts in the job or at home or physical illness. A woman after having a baby can have _postpartum_ depression. She suddenly realizes her role and lifestyle are changed.

Desire For Sex Diminishes

Depression can bring about impotence in the male and frigidity in the female. While the capacity for an erection generally does not diminish in a state of depression . . . the desire for sexual intercourse may diminish. And there may be changes in sexual behavior.

Hysteria

The Origin Of Hysterectomy

The word *hysteria* is derived from the Greek word for uterus. In recent years *hysterectomy* became a popular form of surgery. This is surgery where the uterus is removed. In a negative context, it was thought that the best way to correct female complaints was to perform a hysterectomy.

In ancient days, hysteria was thought to be caused by a wandering uterus.[1] Many believe that hysteria may be caused by sexual conflicts.

Hysteria is an illness which occurs mostly in women, less often in men. It may be evidenced by easy laughing and crying episodes of emotionalism without any apparent explanation. The hysterical patient may relieve his anxiety through a physical illness. The patient may develop amnesia, blurred vision, loss of appetite, loss of sexual desire *(libido)*.

During pregnancy, an hysterical patient may vomit throughout her entire 9 months.

[1]M. I. Weintraub, Hysteria: A Clinical Guide To Diagnosis (Clinical Symposia) 29(6), 1977.

The individual may experience numbness in his hands and legs. This is called *"stocking and glove"* hysteria.

Encourages Sexual Difficulties

In those women who were diagnosed as suffering from hysteria, 86% had sexual difficulties of which 73% claimed they derived no sexual pleasures from intercourse. They stated their vagina was as though it was anesthetized and they had no pleasurable feeling from the act.[1]

Marital difficulties and divorce are quite common among women who may be classed as having hysteria.

The sexual response of persons with hysteria vary. Some women may function normally in the act of sexual intercourse. Others may accommodate their husband to sustain the marriage. This accommodation by the frigid wife is one where she simply offers her body as a vessel to receive and relieve her husband's desires.

On the other hand the wife may become a nymphomaniac. *Nymphomania* is an abnormally excessive sexual desire in the female.

---

[1] J. J. Purtell, E. Robins, M. E. Cohen, Observations On Clinical Aspects of Hysteria (Journal of the American Medical Association) 146:902-909, 1951.

8

HOW PRESCRIPTION DRUGS AFFECT SEX

Affect
Varies
From
Person to
Person

Drugs affect various people in various ways because of biological factors such as: absorption rate, body weight, dosage, interaction with other drugs the individual may be taking. A chart appears in this book which defines some of the common drugs in use today and their effect.

Diuretics

Desire
For Sex
Reduced

Diuretics are prescribed to increase the urinary secretion of water and sodium. They are often given for treatment of high blood pressure *(hypertension)*. The use of diuretics by some men may cause sexual dysfunction which could bring about impotency. In men or women it can reduce the desire for sex.

Breast Tenderness A Side Effect

The diurectic *spironolactone* (commercially known as Aldactone) does have as a possible side effect decreased sexual desire in males and impotence. For females it can generate irregular menses *(periods)*, absence of menstruation *(amenorrhea)* and postmenopausal bleeding. The woman may also experience breast tenderness which could cause her to react to sexual intercourse in a frigid manner. When the drug is stopped, sexual desires and potency generally return to normal.

Blood Pressure—Lowering Drugs (Non-Diuretic)

Discourages Sexual Arousal

The drug *Alpha-methyldopa* is one of the most widely prescribed drugs used to treat high blood pressure. It is more commonly known as Aldomet (and in Canada, as: Dopamet, Medimet or Novomedopa).

In men it can affect sexual function by decreasing libido (the desire for sexual intercourse) and impotence. In women it can also decrease libido, make it difficult for the woman to become sexually aroused and possibly create frigidity with the loss of orgasm.

The male may also experience a delayed ejaculation.

Medically it is believed the drug may relate to catecholamine[1] depletion in the central nervous system and may have a direct effect on the peripheral nerves that control the process of erection and vaginal vasocongestion . . . according to the authors of Textbook of Sexual Medicine.

Secondary Causes

The loss of sex drive may be due to the fact that this drug causes drowsiness and fatigue and sometimes, depression . . . which can encourage sexual difficulties. Other high blood pressure drugs can cause sexual problems.

Guanethidine (Ismelin) can cause a retarded ejaculation or make the male unable to ejaculate. Sexual problems may also be encountered by women.

Hydralazine (Apresoline, Dralzine, Hydralyn, NorPres 25, Rolazine) at doses above 200 mg. per day may decrease the sex drive and can cause impotence.

Encourages Depression

Reserpine (Serpasil; in Canada, Neo-Serp, Reserfia, Reserpanca) may bring about depression which decreases the sex drive and causes sexual dysfunction such as impotence and frigidity. It may also cause *gynecomastia* (abnormally large mammary glands in the male) or *galactorrhea* (continuation of flow of milk from the breasts of

---

[1]*Catecholamine* is an amino acid derivative that has a marked effect on the nervous and cardiovascular systems, metabolic rate, temperature and smooth muscle.

the female after the stopping of nursing or excessive flow of milk).

**Can
Cause
Impotence**

Propranolol (Inderal) has been reported by some doctors to cause impotence.[1]

Clonidine (Catapres) has been reported by some in the medical field to cause a decrease in the sex drive and, in some cases, impotence in men.[2]

Boehringer Ingelheim Ltd., producers of Catapres state that in 1,923 patients given Catapres, impotence and/or loss of libido occurred in 53 (2.8%).

Captopril (Capoten) is a new drug produced by Squibb Corporation for the treatment of high blood pressure. While it is too early to fully assess, it is being offered as a substitute for other anti-hypertensive drugs because it does not have the side effects other existing medications have—fatigue, depression and impotence.

Prazosin (Minipress) causes a decreased sex drive in about 15% of the men and women taking this drug, although impotence infrequently occurs.[3]

---

[1]R. A. Miller, Propranolol And Impotence (letter). Annals of Internal Medicine 85-682-683, 1976. Also, S. C. and S. G. Warren, Ibid., 86:112, 1977.

R. C. Kolodny, Antihypertensive Drugs and Male Sexual Function. Presented at the Eleventh National Sex Institute, Washington, D.C., April 1, 1978.

[2]Robert E. Kolodny, M.D., William H. Masters, M.D., Virginia E. Johnson, D.Sc. (Hon.), Textbook of Sexual Medicine (Boston: Little, Brown and Company) 1979, p. 325.

[3]Ibid., p. 325.

9

SEX AND HORMONE THERAPY

**Sensitivity
Increases**

Sex hormones act on the penis in the male and the vagina of the female to enhance their sensitivity and responsiveness.

Androgens are substances producing or stimulating male characteristics as the male sex hormone . . . _testosterone_.

The hormone responsible for the sexual response in both men and women appears to be largely the male hormone, testosterone.

The female hormones (_estrogen and progesterone_) are not as important factors in the human female's sex drive. They are, of course, essential in ovulation and pregnancy.

If a man has normal testosterone production, the adding of Androgens does not increase either potency or sex drive.

**Continued
Use
Harmful**

However, continued intake of Androgen (adrenal sex hormones) may cause the testicles to become reduced in size and the sperm diminish its fertility.

Male atheletes who take Androgen-type steroids in large quantities become infertile. Androgen therapy may also bring prostate enlargement and other associated risks.

In men with low testosterone (the male sex hormone), androgen therapy can often restore the sex drive and potency.

Androgen therapy can also bring behavioral changes increasing "*aggression*" as well as one's energy level and appetite. A mild-mannered individual may become less timid and more forthright with discernable personality changes.

Androgen and Women

**Triggers
Sex
Center**

Androgen hormone therapy also triggers the sex centers in women. When a woman has a low androgen-estrogen ratio, the adding of testosterone is highly effective as an aphrodisiac.[1]

Women who have surgical removal of their ovaries and adrenals lose all their sexual desire. They no longer have erotic dreams nor can they be sexually stimulated to arousal. However, when they receive the

---

[1]Aphrodisiac *is an agent or drug which stimulates sexual desire.*

Androgen hormone in therapy they become highly aroused sexually.

Cannot Be Used During Pregnancy

Androgen therapy cannot be used on pregnant women because of risk to the fetus (if the fetus is female). Then, too, while the adding of high doses of androgen increases the sex drive in women, it can also produce side effects. These side effects include:

1. Excessive growth of hair or the presence of hair in unusual places (Hirsutism)
2. Acne
3. Clitoral enlargement
4. Sodium retention

It is for these reasons that caution must be exercised when the male sex hormone, androgen, is administered in order to make the impotent male potent and the frigid woman sexually responsive.

Estrogen and Men

Brings Impotence

Estrogen is often used in the treatment of cancer of the prostate in men. When such therapy is used the sex drive is lessened and usually impotence is the end result. The reason for this is that the estrogen reduces the production of the male sex hormone, testosterone.

It also affects the male's ability to have a complete, full ejaculation because the volume of seminal fluid is reduced. If estrogen therapy continues in a male, he develops abnormally large breasts which sometimes secrete milk (Gynecomastia). Facial hair growth also slows down.

Estrogen and Women

Changes Occur With Age

While some women have the good fortune to experience menopause without any recognizable symptoms ... most women do have definable changes in their hormone structure. These may include:

1. Vasomotor instability *(hot flashes)*
2. Irritability or Depression
3. Aging changes in the breasts, genitals and skin

Suddenly when attempting intercourse, the husband may discover that his wife's vagina is dry or has little lubrication. He may mistake this as a sign that his wife is frigid ... when actually she is going through the stage of menopause.

Vaginal lubrication occurs within 10 to 30 seconds after initiation of sexual stimulation. The clitoris may become erect and the vagina begins to enlarge and balloon to accommodate the penis.

Vaginal Tube Shrinks

As the woman reaches her menopausal years (usually between the ages of 40 and 50), the vaginal tube shrinks. It is the vaginal canal or tube which accommodates the penis. The walls of the vagina may also lose their elasticity.

As this aging process continues (because of estrogen deficiency) the breasts of the woman begin to droop. If the woman's health is good, aging will not necessarily

SEX AND HORMONE THERAPY

decrease her sex drive or her capacity to have an orgasm during sexual intercourse.

Controversial Therapy

ERT (Estrogen Replacement Therapy) given to counteract decreasing estrogen levels during menopause is considered a controversial therapy.

Some in the health field believe that estrogen therapy brings an increased risk of breast cancer and cancer of the uterus *(Endometrial cancer)*. It can bring vaginal bleeding, breast tenderness, abdominal bloating, uterine cramps and nausea. To minimize risks most medical authorities recommend it only be given for *"hot flashes"* and inflammation of the vaginal canal *(atrophic vaginitis)*. When given, it is usually given in very low doses.

SEX AND TRANQUILIZERS, SEDATIVES

Reduce Sex Hormone Effectiveness

Tranquilizers such as *chlordiazepoxide hydrochloride* (Librium) and *diazepam* (Valium) both have a host of side effects. Either of these drugs may increase or decrease the sex drive.

Sedatives *(barbiturates)* produce a central nervous system depression and reduce the action of androgen on the male sex hormone altering the levels of testosterone and estrogen. Generally the use of barbiturate sedatives decreases the sex drive. It can bring impotence to the male and frigidity to the female.

10

SEX AND ADDICTIVE SUBSTANCES

**Alcohol
Depresses
Desires**

Alcohol is a general brain depressant. The depressant works in stages. Initially, alcohol depresses the brain centers which govern fear. After a drink or two an otherwise sexually conservative individual can lose all their inhibitions and quickly become sexually active.

Larger doses of alcohol rapidly depress sexual desire. Chronic alcoholism can lead to impotence or frigidity. The man will experience difficulty having an erection ... the woman will lose interest in sexual intercourse.

SEX AND CIGARETTES

**May
Suppress
Sex Hormone**

Recent studies have shown there is a link between cigarette smoking and an early onset of menopause[1] and cancer of the cervix.[2]

Conflicting tests show that in some cases cigarette smoking suppresses the sex hormone *testosterone*. If this is true, it could

[1]H. Jick, J. Porter, A. S. Morrison, Relation Between Smoking And Of Natural Menopause (Lancet) 1977, 1:1354-1355.

[2]R. R. Williams, J. W. Horm, Association Of Cancer Sites With Tobacco And Alcohol Consumption (Journal of The National Cancer Institute) 1977, 58:525-547.

lead to the sexual problems of impotence or frigidity.

Aside from the dangers of taking into your system the many poisonous chemicals of nicotine, tar, etc., cigarette smoking directly causes sexual problems.

Does Not Encourage Sexual Relations

Sexual intercourse requires the greatest of intimacy. One can get no closer to one's mate. If one partner is a non-smoker the intimate relationship can easily be turned off by stale tobacco breath or a room filled with smoke.

Then, too, the artificial high that cigarette smoking gives temporarily places the individual on a high/low energy seesaw. This is another deterrent to frequent sex.

It is these side effects that can decrease the sex drive and encourage both impotence and frigidity in later years.

A Revealing Study

A 14-year study was made by Dr. Takeshi Hirayama of Tokyo. The study involved about 143,000 women and 122,000 men. The research concluded that wives of smokers were 2.08 times more likely to contract lung disease than wives of nonsmokers.

The Tobacco Institute, lobbying arm of the American tobacco industry, alleged that an error in calculations rendered Hirayama's conclusions invalid. But Hirayama said he used a standardized computer program developed at the National Cancer Institute in

Washington. He stood by his findings when he released his report in June, 1981. As an interesting sidelight, medical reports show that heavy smokers may shorten their life as much as 8 years off their potential life-span. Smoking also encourages coronary heart disease, lung cancer and chronic bronchitis.

If the Hirayama report is accurate it is easy to see that a non-smoking spouse may eventually be affected sexually by a smoking partner in what appears initially as a hidden illness.

SEX AND MARIJUANA, LSD, COCAINE

**A
False
Promise**

Those who push illicit drugs often sing the praises that such drugs will give you a sexual high. This is not true. Because they realize that men and women seek to increase their sexual drive, they make this false claim to push more drugs. By the time the individual realizes the claim is false . . . he is already hooked on drugs!

Marijuana

**Affects
Sexual
Glands**

In numerous studies the use of marijuana has brought about a decrease in the desire for sexual intercourse depressing the levels of the male sex hormone, testosterone.

In females, marijuana adversely affects the pituitary gland suppressing the milk mechanism in the breasts.

**Did Not
Improve
Erection**

In men, according to one study, marijuana can produce unusually large breasts in men . . . breasts which even produce milk *(gynecomastia).*[1] With continual marijuana use the testosterone level becomes so low that the male becomes impotent.

In studies made by Masters & Johnson Institute the majority of men and women interviewed stated that marijuana did not increase their sexual desire nor their inten-

[1]J. Harmon, M. A. Aliapoulos, Gynecomastia In Marijuana Users (New England Journal of Medicine) 1972, 287:936.

In females, marijuana adversely affects the pituitary gland suppressing the milk mechanism in the breasts. Marijuana does not increase sexual desire or intensity of orgasm.

sity of orgasm. The men stated marijuana did not increase the firmness of their erection, nor did it make it easier for them to get an erection. The women stated marijuana did not increase the amount of vaginal lubrication nor did it allow them to be orgasmic more frequently. The study covered 800 men and 500 women who were marijuana users between the ages of 18 and 30.

Discourages Intercourse

Most people interviewed said that if their sexual partner was not "high" at the same time as they were, the effect was unpleasant rather than enjoyable. Many users connect sex with marijuana because the drug encourages an increased sense of touch and a greater degree of relaxation. However, it also relaxes the individual to the point of sleeping . . . which is not the ideal state for sexual intercourse.

LSD

Short Circuits Brain

LSD is a powerful hallucinogen.[1] Images and thoughts become vivid and out of proportion because normal brain transmissions are short-circuited. In this state of mental intoxication, sexual intercourse no longer is an erotic experience, but simply a "different" experience.

[1]Hallucinogen is to wander in the mind giving a false perception which has no relation to reality.

Heroin and Methadone

Sex Hormone Lowers

Heroin and Methadone users find themselves with a lowering of the male sex hormone, testosterone and thus a lessening of the sex drive. In tests made with male Heroin users, more than half had a lower sex drive and were impotent. Most of the others had a delayed ejaculation time. Heroin addiction also lowers pituitary gonadotropin levels which directly affects the genitals.

T. J. Cicero and his coworkers reported that the sex drive (libido) decreased substantially in both heroin addicts and users of methadone. They also noted there was a high rate of either retarded ejaculation or even failure to ejaculate.[1]

Women who use heroin or methadone have been reported to have a decreased sex drive, cessation of menstruation, infertility, abnormal milk flow from breasts. And in one study, 30% of the women had a reduction in their breast size.[2]

[1] T. J. Cicero, R. D. Bell, W. G. Wiest, J. H. Allison, K. Polakoski, E. Robins, Function Of The Male Sex Organs In Heroin And Methadone Users (New England Journal of Medicine) 1975, 292:882-887.

[2] J. Bai, E. Greenwald, H. Caterini, H. A. Kaminetzky, Drug-related Menstrual Aberrations (Obstetrics and Gynecology) 1974, 44:713-719.

Cocaine

**Does Not
Intensify
Orgasm**

Cocaine is a white crystalline powder obtained from the cocoa plants in South America. It acts in much the way amphetamines act by inducing wakefulness, a mild euphoria and a loss of appetite.

Any increased sex awareness is very brief. Its reputation of improving firmness and durability of erection and intensifying orgasm for both men and women does not stand up to tests made. Cocaine more frequently causes loss of erection and even priapism. *Priapism is an abnormal, painful and continued erection of the penis due to disease, usually without sexual desire.*

Amphetamine

**Drug
Enslaves
User
To
Dependence**

Amphetamine is a centrally acting brain stimulant. It has been used to control appetite in treating obesity but has not proven effective. Large doses are toxic and prolonged use causes drug dependence. Some Amphetamine users claim it enhances their sexual experiences and they cannot perform wihout it. The truth is that they have become addicted and cannot function in any capacity without it. The amphetamine addicted person is usually very sick emotionally and sexual interests are not enhanced but rather diminished.

Use of any of these drugs shows an emotional and mental imbalance. In most cases the individual seeks to escape from reality and blames society, his family, husband or wife for the problems of the world.

Encourages Impotence And Frigidity

Use of drugs encourages both impotence in the male and frigidity in the female. Like the elusive pot of gold at the end of the rainbow ... the drug user seeks a *"greater than great"* sex life with continual ecstatic climaxes of repeated orgasms. But the drugs give the individual an initial vibrant experience. From then on ... all is down hill. Impotence and Frigidity become their pot of gold!

11

SEX AND THE HANDICAPPED

**A Question
Of
Outlook**

In an article in Postgraduate Medicine, Anderson and Cole give some interesting observations they convey to those that are handicapped:

> A stiff penis does not make a
>   solid relationship,
>   nor does a wet vagina.
> Urinary incontinence
>   does not mean genital incompetence.
> Absence of sensation
>   does not mean absence of feelings.
> Inability to move
>   does not mean inability to please.
> The presence of deformities
>   does not mean the absence of desire.
> Inability to perform
>   does not mean inability to enjoy.
> Loss of genitals
>   does not mean loss of sexuality.[1]

Spinal Cord-Injured Patient

**Erection
Possible**

In the male patients with spinal cord injuries almost 90% could achieve erections. These are termed *reflexogenic erections* and are erections which occur when the penis is touched, tactile stimulation. Of this 90%, 4% could ejaculate. Reflexogenic

---

[1]T. P. Anderson, T. M. Cole, Sexual Counseling Of The Physically Disabled (Postgraduate Medicine) 1975, 58:117-123.

erections are often extremely brief in duration. Usually, they do not produce physical sensations for the man.

The rate of erection is higher with men whose injury is higher in the spinal cord. Only about 20% of the men surveyed with spinal cord injury were able to have a sufficient erection to have sexual intercourse. Few could ejaculate.

Other Areas Become Sexually Responsive

In a Masters & Johnson research the sexual responses of women were tested who were in good health. One woman in particular derived little erotic pleasure from breast stimulation. However, after she sustained an injury which left her paralyzed from the waist and below, she found that her breasts became increasingly sensitive to erotic stimulation. She even developed orgasms as a result of breast stimulation.

In the Textbook of Sexual Medicine, the report relates that as the intensity of breast stimulation increased:

> ... the lips of the woman's mouth became engorged to twice their normal size.
>
> At the moment of orgasm, a pulsating wave was observed in her lips and the swelling then dissipated rapidly.
>
> This illustrates the ability to transfer erotic zones from one region of the body to another.[1]

[1]Robert E. Kolodny, M.D., William H. Masters, M.D., Virginia E. Johnson, D.Sc. (Hon.), Textbook of Sexual Medicine (Boston: Little, Brown and Company) 1979, p. 368.

**Fertility
Impaired**

Men with spinal cord injury have impaired fertility although the male sex hormone, testosterone, is usually normal. Women, on the other hand, experience little reduction in fertility. Successful pregnancies with vaginal delivery are common. Caesarean section is not usually required.

It is understandable that spinal cord injuries can lead to both impotence and frigidity. However, if the partners communicate freely with each other their needs and desires . . . this potential barrier can be successfully overcome.

12

SEX AND RAPE

Affects
Women
Two Ways

Rape is *illicit sexual intercourse without consent*. Rape is a violent assault upon a woman in which sex is used as a weapon. Rape can affect a woman both physically and psychologically.

In the United States, one rape is <u>reported</u> every 7 minutes! It is the fastest-growing violent crime. Reported rapes occur at the rate of about 200 per day or 62,500 per year in the U.S. But keep this in mind. This is just the tip of the iceberg. *It is estimated that 90% of the assaults are never reported!*

No
Age
Limit

Victims of rape have been from as young as 2 <u>months</u> to as old as 97 years! The age group most affected are the 10-19-year-olds. The Nurse's Reference Library reports:

The average victim's age is 13½.
Over 50% of rapes occur in the home;
　About 1/3rd involve a male intruder,
　who forces his way into a home.
Approximately half the time,
　the victim has some casual acquaint-
　ance with the attacker.
Most rapists are 15-24 years old.
Usually the attack is planned . . .

Victims who articulate their feelings
are able to cope with fears,
interact with others,
and return to normal routines
faster than those who do not.[1]

Shy Away From Sex

D. Metzger, herself a victim of rape, describes the rape victim's reaction as a total loss of self . . . leading to a sense of emptiness and isolation from society.[2]

In one study, women who had been raped, exhibited anxiety, depression and some turned to lesbianism.[3] Many rape victims shy away from further sexual encounters and enter marriage with hidden fears. These fears include loss of self-esteem, guilt, fear of rejection by the sexual partner, anger toward men in general.

Intercourse Arousal Difficult

After marriage these women may experience loss of any genital sensation with their husband. Their husband may find difficulty in sexually arousing them. Vaginal lubrication may be limited. The woman

---

[1]Diseases, Causes and Diagnosis (Horsham, Pennsylvania: Intermed Communications) 1981, p. 172.

[2]D. Metzger, It Is Always The Woman Who Is Raped (American Journal of Psychiatry) 1976, 133:405-408.

[3]Lesbianism is the sexual desire of women for one of their own sex.

may experience pain during intercourse and loss of any orgasm. Outwardly, she may convey sexual satisfaction to her husband by faking erotic thrills and orgasm. Eventually, unless there is communication and counselling, she can become frigid.

Long Lasting Effects

One popular female singer of the 1960's was raped in her motel room. The experience was so traumatic that she became frigid for many years.

One of the hidden causes of frigidity is that the woman at some time in life was raped. This frightening episode can have long-lasting effects which may not surface for years.

Along with rape as a cause for later frigidity . . . is also pedophilia. A Pedophiliac *is a person who has sexual relations with children.* The child can subconsciously harbor this experience for life. It can affect sexual responsiveness in the married years.

If 90% of the rape cases are never reported (and there are 62,500 reported rape cases per year) . . . total rapes in the U.S. could approach well over 1/2 Million women each year. This means in 10 years, some 5 Million women have been raped. One can see how several million marriages can be affected with women becoming frigid.

13

HOW EMOTIONS CAUSE SEX FAILURE

Concern Over Sexual Functions

There are what is called _psychogenic_ causes for impotence. Psychogenic means _of mental origin_.

Many problems of impotence and frigidity occur because the individual has an involuntary tendency to exert conscious control over the orgasmic reflex, reports Helen Singer Kaplan, M.D. This concern over one's sexual performance becomes so intense that it hinders the mechanisms for a fulfilling sexual intercourse. The mind exerts a strong influence over the actions and reactions of the body. What develops is sexual conflict.

With liberated women who expect more from their men in today's permissive and fast-paced society, the male has developed a _"performance anxiety."_ Impotence, once a problem of the middle age, is now also a growing problem among young people!

RELIGION And SEX

"Unfortunately, 50% of marriages in America today have problems stemming largely from ignorance in the area of sexual adjustment," so says Dr. J. Jones Stewart.

Dr. Stewart has been a practicing physician for over 41 years. He is a specialist in the fields of obstetrics, gynecology and sexual therapy. He has pioneered in the field of human sexuality. His father was a Southern Baptist minister. Dr. Stewart has a Baptist background and is a member of an Independent Congregationalist church in California.

He gives lectures on human sexuality in many churches. Much of his practice is directed to those who come from *"born again"* Christian backgrounds. There are some 60 million Americans who claim a biblical Christianity religious experience.

Sexual problems in these circles arise because parents from an orthodox religious background fail to give good sex education to their children. As many wives as husbands come to him because they find a lack of sexual fulfillment.

Dr. Stewart feels that much of the problems of sex that married people have is because of a restrictive religious upbringing that was based on pseudo-religious standards. Parents who believe the Bible and instruct their children in its precepts are sometimes reluctant to discuss sex. Instead they pass on to their children traditional sexual myths which have no basis in the Bible itself! Dr. Stewart suggests such people read and study the Song of Solomon in the Old Testament.

Thus, even marriages between Bible-believers can fall on rocky times because they find it an embarrassment to discuss sexual needs. Dr. Stewart believes: *"If in good health, there's nothing to hinder a married couple from experiencing good sexual activity and sexual enjoyment during their entire life span."* Dr. Stewart sees no reason why sex should be practiced only until you reach 50 or 60 or 70.[1]

---

[1]J. Jones Stewart, M.D., <u>Tell Me Doctor</u> (Rosemead, California: Psychology For Living) Narramore Christian Foundation, June, 1981, pp. 14, 15.

Three Fears

Men are faced with three basic fears:

1. Fear of failure
   Called upon to sexually perform, the male may be so emotionally concerned with getting his penis to an erection that this fear brings failure. Once there is a failure, the next opportunity for sexual intercourse will harbor a continuing fear ... unless the wife can properly counsel and stimulate her husband to sexual arousal.

2. Sex on demand
   The *"new liberated woman,"* reports Dr. Kaplan, has high expectations and demands for sexual performance.[1] Sex is demanded as proof of commitment and love. The wife may demand sexual intercourse at night when the husband is weary and tired. He finds himself unable to perform. His wife interprets this as lack of love for her. If such pressure continues, the male can become impotent leading eventually also to frigidity in the female. The wife may further accent the problem by saying, *"Am I getting too old for you? Don't you love me any more?"*

Different Times

If a husband shows signs of impotence, the wife should consider performing the sexual act at other times during the day. She should also consider different positions for intercourse. There is nothing more deadly to a marriage than routine. The same sexual position, the same time

[1]Helen Singer Kaplan, M.D., Ph.D., The New Sex Therapy (New York: Times Books) 1974, p. 262.

of day or evening, the quick performance ... all can lead to either impotence or frigidity in later years.

3. The Inability of Abandonment

An Uncluttered Mind Essential

A husband can tend towards impotence if he is unable to completely abandon himself freely to the sexual act. If his mind is preoccupied with other thoughts or if he becomes concerned about his ability to perform ... he may have difficulty in having an erection or in maintaining one.

Then, too, if his early childhood was restricted as far as a healthy attitude towards marital sex was concerned, his subconscious mind will deter his ability for complete sexual fulfillment.

In a letter to Ann Landers, a wife writes:

I've been married six years and our sex life has deteriorated to almost zero.

Now the roles are reversed.
It is my husband who says,
  "I'm tired,
  I've got too much on my mind,"
and
  "Is that all you think about?"

Role Reversals Threatening

The wife had a high-salaried position and the husband was proud of her accomplishments. But then the husband lost his job and became depressed and frustrated. This emotional crisis triggered a season of impotence in the husband. He was unable to abandon himself for a brief period of sexual union.

His wife concluded:

> Ann, you were right when you said
> "Count your blessings"
> to the women whose husbands
> can't keep their hands off them.
>
> I'd melt if mine would grab me!
> We love each other but are miles apart.
> How can I motivate him to want me
>   as much as I want him?

There are other emotional factors that can affect satisfying sexual relations.

One Parent Dominance

Unbalanced Childhood

A more than usual mother-son relationship over a prolonged period of time can bring about impotence in the male in later years. This undue dominance by the mother can lead to erectile problems in her son because he has no father-dominant figure to measure up to.

This often also brings with it a negative attitude towards wholesome marital sex.

Traumatic First Coital Experience

Early Encounters Can Be Disappointing

The first sexual contact of an individual can be a disturbing one because he or she is not emotionally equipped to handle it.

Violations of Biblical principals bring with them eventual penalties.

Pre-marriage sex under adverse circumstances and pressured conditions motivates a male to have quick ejaculation. He may ejaculate even before he can enter. This initial experience may humiliate him.

Circumstances similar to this, while not visibly seeming important, could in later years surface subconsciously to create problems of impotence.

The girl who is pressured to perform sexually prior to marriage *"to prove your love to me"* or because *"everybody else is doing it"* may experience no pleasure but rather a distaste for the act that has humiliated her. In later years, she may become frigid in her sexual relations with her husband.

Triggered Impotence

Dr. Helen Singer Kaplan relates the interview with a 54-year-old man whose first attempt at coitus at age 17 ended in disaster. He ejaculated before he could enter and his female companion laughed at him. He never saw her again. When he attempted intercourse a second time with another girl, he found himself impotent . . . at age 17. He married a woman who only wanted sex once a month. With this infrequency, he was able to perform. But after a divorce and more demands for sex by his companions, he suffered from secondary impotence.[1]

One parent dominance and traumatic first coital experience are considered developmental factors in emotional impotence or frigidity. Homosexuality is another developmental factor. Homosexual men and women can become heterosexual and function in the way God intended them. Masters and Johnson have had clinical success in this area.

[1] Helen Singer Kaplan, M.D., Ph.D., The New Sex Therapy (New York: Times Books) 1974, p. 178.

14

WHEN THE MARRIAGE BED
BECOMES A BATTLEGROUND

**Personality
Changes**

Sexual dysfunction often is the result of either subsconscious or conscious conflict between husband and wife.

Particularly in today's fast-paced society and mood changing drugs, many men and women have an unsuccessful sex life. This lack of fulfillment in this area can trigger personality changes that make a marriage unstable. Dr. Kaplan notes that there are millions of traumatized women who have never had an orgasm and there are also men who suffer from absolute ejaculatory incompetence ... a condition where the man never ejaculates in his entire life.[1]

Lack of Trust

**Security
A
Prime
Goal**

A wife craves security and release from any tension or stress that would threaten this security. If the home situation is one where the husband does not earn sufficient income to maintain the living standard the wife desires, sexual problems can develop.

[1]Ibid., p. 146.

The wife wants to make sure her husband will remain loyal to her. Perhaps in her childhood years, an unstable home life, financial difficulties, marital discord reinforced her desire to avoid such a problem in her marriage. If there is the hint of them appearing in her marriage, her sexual relations with her husband can be discouraging. It can lead to frigidity.

A One-sided Pleasure

She may accept sexual intercourse with her husband on a regular basis but from an erotic viewpoint, it is one-sided. Because she feels insecure, she will hold back any pleasure she could derive from sexual union. And similarly, her husband sensing this lack of responsiveness, may become both frustrated and angry. And this could trigger impotence.

Then, too, if the partner can accept the fact that he cannot achieve an erection every time or she cannot experience an orgasm ... this communication of understanding will go a long way to establishing a healthy trust relationship.

Power Dominance

Inner Conflicts Develop

There may be an unconscious desire for either the husband or the wife to completely dominate the other spouse. The wife, who previous to marriage, had a good education and her eyes set on a career ...

suddenly finds herself married and pregnant. Her husband dominates her both in sexual positions and in his attitude. This power struggle causes an inner conflict. She develops an inner hostility. She finds herself tied down to responsibilities at home while her husband has free movement without being concerned about who is going to feed the baby, etc.

A Subtle Revenge

The one way the wife can become "*victor*" over the power struggle is to refuse to have an orgasm. Be relinquishing this pleasure she gains satisfaction in her power struggle.

In today's society where more women are working and some earning more than their husbands . . . the husband may sense a lack of potency because he is not indispensable. This role reversal may bring on impotency.

Then, too, to insure power dominance or power equality the woman may withhold sex to gain certain concessions from her husband. An erection is an involuntary nervous system reflex. It is impossible to will an erection to occur. And where there is an emotional struggle between partners (either conscious or subsconscious) such a struggle may bring about impotence in the male.

To demonstrate her power dominance, during initial lovemaking, she may tell him that she expects him to have an instant erection. Such a demand will emotionally make him incapable of performing.

15

FULFILLING YOUR PARTNER'S DESIRES

**A
Rhythm
Of
Life**

Body time is a subject in itself. There is a rhythm of life. A study of this rhythm is a new branch of biology which deals with *circadian cycles*. There are 24-hour rhythms as well as other cycles such as the monthly menstrual cycle.

Premenstrual tension usually occurs four to five days just before onset of menses. Some 60% of women will experience perhaps mild irritation, depression, headache or a decline in attentiveness. Some women may have very strong sexual desires at this time while others may have diminished desire.

**Male
Mood
Changes**

Men also have a rhythmic change although it may be less conspicuous. Dr. Christian Hamburger, a Danish endocrinologist analyzed his own urine for 16 years to see how the sex hormones were affected by gonadal secretion. He discovered that there was a near-monthly rhythm . . . patterned after the monthly rhythm of women.[1]

---

[1]Gay Gaer Luce, Body Time (New York: Pantheon Books) 1971, pp. 237, 238.

**Bad
Timing
Discourages
Sex**

Understanding this, either a husband or wife can make demands on lovemaking at a time when the other partner is not in the mood. This continual demanding and bad timing can lead to sexual dysfunction. The reason: Occasional rebuffs by either spouse (if there is lack of honest sexual communication) can grow out of proportion where the husband becomes impotent or the wife becomes frigid.

The husband may want to make love when the wife has a pile of dishes to do, or the children need her attention . . . or after she has received a distressing phone call.

Or the wife may be anxious for sex when her husband is tired from a particularly trying day at work or is trying to sort out emotional or health problems that plague him.

The key to a fulfilling sex life is complete and mutual understanding of the marriage partners where one's feelings are discussed in complete honesty.

The Slob and Sex

**Soap
Is
Cheap**

The word *"slob"* is not a refined word but it quite graphically describes the problem of one who is sloppy, coarse or crude.

Of the 7,239 men who responded to a survey taken by Shere Hite only 3% mentioned orgasm as the reason they liked sexual intercourse. The most common responses cited the physical closeness, sensations of masculinity, acceptance and love.

Sexual intercourse is the closest way to express the deepest forms of love ... when two bodies are actually united as one.

Understanding this, how important it is that each partner approach this act in the most appealing, loving fashion. A husband who is fat, who smokes cigars, and only takes a bath once a week will hardly turn on a wife. This is particularly true if the wife watches her weight, bathes daily and is scrupulous about her hairstyle and clothes she wears. She can easily become frigid.

And it is no surprise if the man becomes impotent if he has to go to bed each night with a wife who has body odor because of infrequent bathing, who has not brushed her teeth and whose hair is up in curlers.

Grooming Important

Grooming will go a long way to a happier sex life. Any man who is not turned on by the sight of his wife lying in bed in a frilly, transparent nightgown, bathed and waiting to make love ... most likely has a sexual dysfunction.

If you are impotent or frigid, examine your lifestyle from a grooming standpoint.

Fulfilling the Partner's Desires

Deferring To One Another Vital

The sexual response in marriage will become much more fulfilling if both husband and wife seek to comply with the other's legitimate desires. Just as tastes in food differ with husband and wife, so does the approach to sexual union.

**Wife
Must Be
Satisfied
Also**

The husband may like to plunge in immediately and quickly ejaculate. The wife desires an initial period of foreplay and some romanticism.

The wife may have special areas of her back and buttocks she wants tickled to arouse her sexually. He may wish simply to touch and manipulate her nipples.

The wife may like to move her hips as the sexual climax causes uncontrollable pulsation. He may wish her to remain still while he ejaculates and pin her down so she is immobile.

The man may crave oral sex. The wife may be repelled by the thought.

The woman may want clitoral stimulation so she can have an orgasm. The man may think that the _missionary position_[1] is the only proper way for orgasm.

Continued frustration by husband or wife in not having one's sexual desires met can lead to impotence and frigidity.

---

[1]The missionary position _is where the man lies full length on top of the woman with his penis inserted from the front._ It is the male-dominant/woman-passive position and is the one most commonly used.

16

THE MALE AND PREMATURE EJACULATION

Two More Male Problems

Throughout the beginning of this book we have discussed some of the reasons and solutions to the problem of impotence. Impotence has been defined as *the inability of the man to perform the sex act because of failure to achieve or sustain an erection sufficient to complete intercourse.*

There are two other male sexual dysfunctions: Premature Ejaculation and Retarded Ejaculation.

PREMATURE EJACULATION

Beyond Voluntary Control

Premature ejaculation (*ejaculatio praecox*) basically is a condition where the husband is unable to exert voluntary control over the reflex action that brings about ejaculation. With this condition, once the male is sexually aroused, he reaches orgasm and ejaculates very quickly.

To define premature ejaculation exactly is difficult for it would vary from couples to couples . . . depending on the response of the female.

If the wife is able to have her orgasm after her husband has been thrusting in her for 60 seconds ... then the husband's performance would not be considered premature ejaculation.

In some textbooks prematurity is defined as the occurrence of ejaculation 30 seconds after vaginal entry. Others extend the time up to 2 minutes. Dr. Helen Singer Kaplan observes that most premature ejaculators will ejaculate just prior to or immediately upon entering the vagina.

Thus ... premature ejaculation could be considered ejaculation that is <u>beyond man's voluntary control.</u>

Develops Early

Men who have the condition of premature ejaculation usually develop it early in life. These are young men usually with a high sex drive and no difficulty in getting an erection.

However, there are men who develop it as a secondary dysfunction, that is, after a long period of good sexual functioning and ejaculatory control. These men usually are in the older age group and may have difficulties in having an erection. Some sexual therapists place this group as a form of impotence where the capacity to ejaculate is still retained.

Premature ejaculation can come about also in men with an enlarged prostate (*prostatism*).

Anxiety Destroys Performance

Stephen B. Levine, M.D. writes in <u>Medical Times</u>:

Once the man believes he is a
premature ejaculator,
he develops performance anxiety—
    the vigilant preoccupation
        during sex
    with the mechanical
    rather than the emotional
    aspects of the experience.

He soon develops
a two-part strategy
to avoid arousal to ejaculation:

(1) he sets rules for foreplay
which limit the amount of stimulation
(e.g., *"You may touch my penis,*
        but only for five seconds!")

(2) or he may employ a
series of nonerotic thoughts
to occupy his mind during intromission.[1]
This strategem only increases his
tendency to ignore his penile sensations,
which is a big mistake.
He does not enjoy the early sensations
of orgasm
which he is helpless to prevent . . .

Each sexual *"failure"* induces
more performance anxiety.
Soon his partner senses
his lack of emotional involvement
in lovemaking.
Her pleasure diminishes
and he becomes a poor lover,
regardless of his previous capacities.[2]

---

[1]Intromission *is the period of time when the penis is inserted into the vagina during sexual intercourse.*

[2]Stephen B. Levine, M.D., <u>Male Sexual Problems</u> (New York: Medical Times) June, 1981, p. 13s.

**Mutual
Timing
Essential**

The wife is usually slower to respond during sexual intercourse. Therefore, for her husband to be an effective lover he must be able to continually thrust even while he is in a highly aroused state until both achieve mutual orgasm. Or, if this cannot be accomplished ... then either after or before the husband ejaculates, he should take the time to bring his wife to orgasm by manual stimulation of her clitoris.[1]

While a husband who is young will ejaculate quickly, a young wife will take longer to reach a high plateau of excitement that brings about her orgasm. This is why young married couples rarely experience orgasm simultaneously.

On the other hand, as they get older (in their 40's and 50's), the husband's ejaculation will take longer and the wife's ability to achieve orgasm will become shorter. This may be part of the reasoning that gave birth to the saying: *"Life begins at 40!"*

**Misunderstandings
Can
Develop**

If the young husband is a premature ejaculator, he may try various efforts to avoid intense excitement. His wife may misinterpret these actions as one of rejection. A vicious cycle can develop. Young and inex-

---

[1]*Clitoris is part of the female genitalia. It is an erectile part, located at the top of the outer rim of the vagina. It is surrounded by a fold of skin known as the clitoral hood. During intercourse, the penis tends to move the labia minora, which causes the clitoral hood to move and thus stimulates the clitoris. The clitoris resembles a miniature penis, and is made of the same erectile tissue and is just as sensitive.*

perienced with a lack of husband-wife frank communication, their relationship may develop into one of anger and avoidance. Thus a blossoming romance could start to fade with an unsatisfied sex life. If continued, this could encourage impotence in the man and frigidity in the woman.

Aids To Diminish Sensitivity

Premature ejaculators usually seek medical help only in desperation when the wife threatens to leave or divorce him.

Some believe that premature ejaculation is due to excessive sensitivity to erotic stimulation. To diminish sexual sensations some commonly suggested measures include:

1. The use of condoms
2. Applying anesthetic ointments to the penis
3. Tensing of the anal muscles
4. Mental exercises withdrawing attention away from the sexual act
5. Frequent cold showers
6. Masturbation just prior to intercourse
7. Repeated intercourse

These methods may be temporarily successful but in the long run do not answer the problem. Dr. Kaplan believes they do not improve control once intense erotic arousal is achieved. Such measures may work against a proper solution.

Drugs Not The Answer

Some doctors prescribe a low dose of *phenothiazine* (10 mg. Mellaril) an hour before anticipated sexual intercourse. Phenothiazine is an antipsychotic drug which has many side effects. Some possible side effects are: loss of appetite, visual impairment, constipation, diarrhea, dry mouth, difficult urination, change in sex drive with possible impotence. Abrupt withdrawal can cause nausea, dizziness, headache and insomnia. However, 10 mg. is considered a very low dose.

Anxiety does play an important role in the problem of premature ejaculation.

Start/Stop Technique

James Semans, a urologist, suggested in 1956 that premature ejaculation was due to the *"rapid reflex mechanism"* of ejaculation. His theory was that the reflex mechanism should be prolonged. He suggests:

> The wife should stimulate
> her husband's penis
> with her hand, not by her vagina.
>
> When her husband advises her
> that the sensation just prior to
>   ejaculation
> is present,
> she should stop stimulating his penis.
>
> When the sensation subsides,
> her hands should again stimulate
> her husband's erect penis . . .
> stopping again just prior to the point
> of no return . . . when ejaculation
>   would start,
> if she continued.

This start/stop technique of manual stimulation will help *"mature"* the husband's penis where he can withstand prolonged stimulation within his wife's vagina.

Dr. Semans treated 8 patients with this technique. Dr. Kaplan, in her book, <u>The</u>

Treating Premature Ejaculation

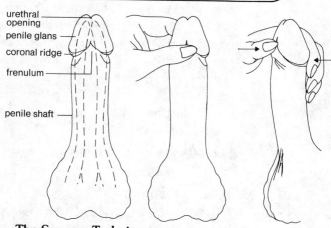

urethral opening
penile glans
coronal ridge
frenulum
penile shaft

The Squeeze Technique

Thumb should be placed on the <u>frenulum</u>.

First and second fingers should be placed just above and below the coronal ridge on the opposite side of the penis. Firm pressure is applied for 4 seconds only ... then quickly released. Never apply pressure from side to side.

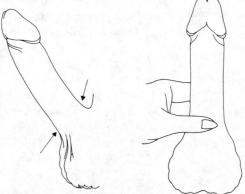

The Basilar Squeeze Technique

Thumb should be placed at base of the penis.

Pressure should be applied ... back to front ... at penis <u>base</u>. Never apply pressure from side to side.

Artwork adapted from medical illustrations by Bob Jackson.

New Sex Therapy, reports that in every case the symptoms of premature ejaculation disappeared within a month.

The Squeeze Technique

Masters and Johnson employ the "*squeeze technique.*" In this procedure, the technique should be practiced several days before sexual intercourse is attempted. The wife squeezes her husband's penis firmly, just below the rim of the glans. She places her thumb on the frenulum of the penis and places her first and second fingers just above and below the coronal ridge on the opposite side of the penis. A firm, grasping pressure is applied for 4 seconds and then abruptly released. The pressure is always applied in a front-to-back fashion, never from side to side. It is important that the woman use the pads of her thumb and fingers and avoid pinching the penis or scratching it with her fingernails.[1]

This reduces the ejaculatory tension. This squeeze technique does not work as well if the husband does it to himself.

Female Superior Position

After several days of practice, the couple is ready to follow through. The husband lies on his back nude. The wife, also nude, sits facing him. The husband's legs should straddle his wife's legs. The wife stimulates her husband's penis until it is erect. She then continues until he indicates that

[1]Robert C. Kolodny, William H. Masters, Virginia E. Johnson, Textbook of Sexual Medicine (Boston: Little, Brown and Company) 1979, p. 525.

ejaculation is imminent. At his signal, the wife stops the stimulation and squeezes his penis. This should cause him to lose his erection partially.

In this same female superior position, the wife should mount her husband, inserting his erect penis into her vagina. The husband should abstain from active thrusting.

After a brief time, when ejaculation is imminent, the wife should move off the penis, apply the squeeze technique again, reinsert his penis into her vagina and begin a slow thrusting pattern. If the husband feels the ejaculation approaching, he signals his wife. She dismounts and uses the squeeze technique again.

Masters and Johnson had success with this technique in 98% of the 186 men treated. The treatment usually took 2 weeks.

The Basilar Squeeze

As a further refinement, the "basilar squeeze" is used after improvements are seen. This technique allows the wife to remain mounted on her husband's penis while she applies pressure-squeeze to the base of his penis. Pressure should be applied back to front at penis base, but not side to side. The base of the penis is the point where it joins the testicles.

Dr. Helen Singer Kaplan is a Clinical Associate Professor of Psychiatry at Cornell University College of Medicine. She also serves as Head of the Sex Therapy and Education Program at the Payne Whitney Clinic of New York Hospital.

**Focus
On
Sensations**

Her technique at Cornell is to get the man to focus his attention repeatedly on the sensations of impending orgasm while he is making love to his partner.

At her clinic, a variation of the Semans "start-stop" method is employed. A preliminary discussion with husband and wife is first on the agenda. Then a series of at-home sessions is suggested:

1. The couple (in their home) engage in limited foreplay that simply brings the husband to erecion.

2. The husband then lies on his back. The wife stimulates his penis. The stimulation can be manually or orally. The husband is told to focus his attention exclusively on the erotic sensations coming from his penis. When he feels ejaculation is imminent, he asks his wife to stop stimulating him. The sensation of impending ejaculation will stop within a few seconds. His wife should then resume stimulation before erection is lost. This "start-stop" procedure should continue for 3 times. On the fourth time, the husband should ejaculate.

3. If the second procedure proves successful, the third approach employs a slight variation. The penis is lubricated with vaseline to closely stimulate the sensations when the penis is in the vagina. Again the husband lies on his back while the wife stimulates his penis manually. Again, he ejaculates on the 4th stimulation.

4. After this is successfully completed, intercourse is suggested in the female superior position. The man puts his hands on the woman's hips. She lowers herself onto his erect phallus and waits for his signal to begin stimulation. The husband lies quietly while he guides and controls his wife's pelvic thrusting with his hands. After this position proves successful, the couple is instructed to attempt intercourse lying on their sides.[1]

A Hidden Fear

Dr. Kaplan reports on one case history where the wife had difficulty in following through on the "*start-stop*" therapy. She had inner fears that once her husband was able to control his premature ejaculation and overcome his sex problems . . . he would become sexually active with other women and abandon her. Her husband reassured her this would not be true.

She was also turned off by the start-stop technique. It encouraged frigidity in her response. To resolve this the husband stimulated her manually while he "*rested*" to prevent premature ejaculation.

[1]Helen Singer Kaplan, M.D., Ph.D., The New Sex Therapy (New York: Times Books) 1974, pp. 305, 306, 307.

17

THE MALE AND RETARDED EJACULATION

**An
Emotional Block**

Ejaculatory incompetence is often referred to as retarded ejaculation *(ejaculatio
retardata)*.

Retarded ejaculation is basically the inability of the male to ejaculate within his wife's
vagina. In fact, he may be unable to ejaculate at all even though his penis is erect.

The difference between impotence and retarded ejaculation is that in impotency the
male generally cannot achieve an erection
of his penis. However, even with a limp
penis, he can ejaculate if he is sufficiently
stimulated. But a limp penis does not
enable him to enter his wife's vagina for
sexual intercourse.

In retarded ejaculation problems, the husband rarely has difficulty getting an erection. In fact he can maintain an erection
for a long period of time during sexual intercourse. He may have an urgent desire to
ejaculate and the stimulation his wife applies to his penis should be more than
enough to trigger the ejaculation ... but
nothing happens.

**Selected
Ejaculation**

The greater problem of retarded ejaculation is where the husband cannot ejaculate into his wife's vagina during normal sexual intercourse. On the other hand, he may easily ejaculate via masturbation or partner manipulation . . . but not in the vagina.

As reported in Medical Times:

> The vagina apparently represents
> a forbidden, dangerous place
> for such a precious organ . . .

> These forms of inhibited orgasm
> may be entirely psychogenic
> and derive from diverse sources:

>   1. Lack of excitement
>   (often seen in married bisexual men)

>   2. Guilt (religious orthodoxy)

>   3. Fear of:

>   A. Embarrassment
>   (Orgasm is seen as an
>   embarrassing loss
>   of control . . .
>   confused with other
>   inappropriate losses—
>   such as loss of bowel control;
>   often seen in
>   obsessive-compulsive
>   personalities;

>   B. Pregnancy

>   C. Injury
>   Usually represents
>   unresolved castration anxiety.[1]

**Can
Become
Chronic**

Retarded ejaculation can be an occasional problem or it can be a chronic problem. Generally only the person who complains

[1]Stephen B. Levine, M.D., Male Sexual Problems (New York: Medical Times) June, 1981, p. 14s.

of never being able to ejaculate seeks advice. He may engage in active sexual intercourse for an hour and still not ejaculate within his wife's vagina. However, when his wife manually manipulates and massages his penis, he will ejaculate. Or if his wife employs oral intercourse by placing his erect penis in her mouth, he will ejaculate.

Thus there is a psychological disturbance that throws a subconscious roadblock on the ejaculatory reflex every time his penis enters his wife's vagina.

Two Conditions

Then, too, there are variations to this problem of retarded ejaculation. The husband may not even be able to ejaculate in the presence of his wife.

Primary retarded ejaculation is where the male noted his inability to ejaculate from his very first sexual intercourse experience. Most of these people can achieve extravaginal orgasm ... that is, ejaculate by means other than sexual intercourse.

Secondary retarded ejaculation is a condition where the male enjoyed a period of good ejaculatory function up to a certain stage in his life when a problem occurred. Some trauma at a point in his life suddenly altered his ability for vaginal ejaculation. He may have been discovered in a forbidden sexual behavior. Or someone may have seen him in the act of sexual intercourse. Whatever the trauma, his subconscious prohibits him from ejaculation into his wife's vagina.

Partial Ejaculatory Incompetence

No Ejaculation Ability

Dr. Helen Singer Kaplan was the first to describe the condition where the ejaculation response is only partially affected.

In partial ejaculatory incompetence, the ability to emit semen is intact. However, the male has no ejaculation ability. In ejaculation there are contractions of about 8/10ths of a second apart in the penis and surrounding muscles. The male may have what can be described as a partial climax but he fails to feel the full throbbing, pulsating sensations that come with complete ejaculation. His semen seeps out from his penis but in this "half" climax it does not spurt out as in normal intercourse.[1]

Condition Usually Temporary

While the husband may be highly interested in sex and have good erections, he will feel his climax approaching but the response will only be the non-pleasurable seepage of seminal fluid. Generally this condition is only temporary and passes and complete sexual fulfillment returns.

Some Causitive Factors

While the condition may be caused by organic factors in some people, it is more often caused by psychological factors. Diabetes, prostatic disease can affect ejaculation.

[1]Helen Singer Kaplan, M.D., Ph.D., The New Sex Therapy (New York: Times Books) 1974, p. 318.

Some drugs can interfere with the sympathetic nervous system. This is particularly true of antipsychotic drugs (such as Mellaril) and some drugs given for high blood pressure (Aldactazide combinations). They may cause *"dry ejaculation"* which is ejaculation without any seminal fluid. (Several fluids are normally present in the ejaculation stream).

A transurethral resection of the prostate is the most common source of the ability to have orgasm without apparent ejaculation. Ejaculation does occur, but into the bladder. This phenomenon is common enough that the patient should be advised of this possibility before surgery.

However, where this is not present, a change of sexual patterns usually brings a solution to the problem. Dr. Kaplan suggests a time be set aside for a pressure-free session of lovemaking, combining intense stimulation with relaxation, and then ending with sexual intercourse and orgasm.

Wife May Misinterpret Lengthly Time

Some husbands, in error, believe that taking a lengthy time to ejaculate is pleasing to the wife since she takes longer to achieve orgasm. However, the wife may interpret this prolonged time to reach any form of ejaculation as evidence of rejection. Some men, to overcome this, will pretend to ejaculate and fake orgasm. This simply prolongs finding the solution to the problem. Eventually the male can become sexually impotent and fail even to gain an erection.

Clinic Approach To Problem

In the Payne Whitney Clinic of New York Hospital, as a general rule, the husband is instructed to engage (in the first 2 or 3 days) in whatever sexual activities he and his wife enjoy. However, he is told not to attempt to ejaculate during this initial period nor to enter his wife's vagina. If he wishes he may bring his wife to orgasm through oral or manual stimulation.

This method of teasing without any demand on the husband to perform, in itself, becomes a powerful sexual stimulant, Dr. Kaplan suggests.

In a progressive, step-by-step program the wife stimulates her husband to the point of impending ejaculation. The husband then inserts his penis into her vagina just as he is about to ejaculate. If the husband fails to ejaculate or loses his erection a special exercise is employed by the wife.

Manual And Vaginal Stimulation

This exercise combines both manual and vaginal stimulation of the husband while both are in the position of intercourse. In the male superior position (sometimes referred to as the *missionary position)* the wife places her right hand under her buttocks. This enables her to stroke and massage the thrusting penis during intercourse. This combination of manual and vaginal and stimulation proves successful in many cases of erectile disorders.

While statistics on retarded ejaculation are few those reported indicate that more than half of those treated at sexual therapy

clinics come away with their problems resolved.

Childhood Experience May Trigger Condition

Because much of the cause of these condi-
itons has its root in an emotional base
which may revert to a childhood experience . . . the husband must seek to discover
what triggered the sexual dysfunction.
Then, too, the wife's actions or reactions to
sex and the methods of sexual intercourse
may have a direct bearing on her husband's
inability to function normally.

In today's fast-paced world, where much of
one's energies are devoted to being financially able to exist in an inflationary
economy .. the male attitude to sex may
be changing. In The Hite Report on Male
Sexuality, nearly a third of the men interviewed said they sometimes had intercourse simply because it seemed to be expected of them.

Many complained about the escalating
pressures to initiate sex, to get and maintain frequent erections, to control the timing of ejaculations and to satisfy their partners' orgasmic needs. Surprising, 51% of
those who said they were having sex daily
also reported masturbating between two
and seven times a week. Could there be a
correlation with increasingly poor nutritional habits that sap the man of sustained
energy?

18

THE FEMALE AND FRIGIDITY

**Frigidity
Not Adequate
Description**

Not much has been written on sexual dysfunctions of the female. Previously these problems have all been lumped under the term "*Frigidity.*"

Frigidity is loosely defined as:

> . . . a coldness and indifference
> to the sexual act
> which results in an inability
> to respond to sexual intercourse
> and to experience sexual pleasure.

The word, frigidity, does not adequately explain the problem that some women have. It conveys that the wife is cold and hostile to her husband. Actually, the wife may be warm and responsive but unable to enjoy or respond to sexual intercourse.

In Kinsey's report on female sexual behavior, 30% of the women did not have orgasms when first married. However, after 10 years of marriage only 10% failed to have orgasms.

In another report with 300 normal women interviewed over a five-year period by Dr. Seymour Fisher . . . 65% of the women preferred clitoral stimulation as opposed to vaginal stimulation. The male superior position encourages clitoral stimulation by the penis. In a large percentage of married couples, clitoral stimulation is done manually.

4 Types

Dr. Helen Singer Kaplan divides female sexual dysfunctions into four distinct syndromes:

1. General sexual dysfunction
2. Orgastic dysfunction
3. Vaginismus
4. Sexual anesthesia

It is very evident when the male is sexually aroused because of the erection of his penis. This is because the blood vessels of the penis become filled with blood.

In the female, sexual arousal indications are more subtle. The principal expression of excitement is swelling of the genitals and lubrication of the vagina. The vaginal area becomes engorged with blood. This is known as *vasocongestion*. The vagina enlarges just enough to hug the penis. The vaginal walls swell up and darken to a deep purple color. The clitoris expands and balloons into an internal erection.

As in the male, the female sexual response consists of involuntary muscle movements. When these movements are impaired in any degree there is female sexual dysfunction.

General Sexual Dysfunction

**No
Erotic
Feeling**

In this condition the female experiences no erotic feelings. The vascular system in her vagina may not function sexually. She does not lubricate nor does her vagina expand to accommodate her husband's penis. She may or may not have an orgasm.

General sexual dysfunction is usually referred to as "frigidity." Some suggest it is the most common of the 4 female sexual dysfunctions. The wife shows no interest in sexual intercourse. It may be to them an ordeal to be endured simply as an accommodation to their husband. Some wives may enjoy the closeness of intercourse but be turned off from the actual act.

**Two
Types**

General sexual dysfunction can be either primary frigidity or secondary frigidity.

In primary frigidity, the woman has never experienced any sexual joy with her husband at any time.

In secondary frigidity, the woman has had sexual arousal at one time but then became frigid later in their marriage.

**Reactions
Differ**

Men and women react differently to sexual dysfunctions. A man who suddenly finds himself unable to have an erection can become highly distrubed, while a frigid woman may simply accept her condition cooly or run the range of emotions to near hysteria.

Sex drive and response

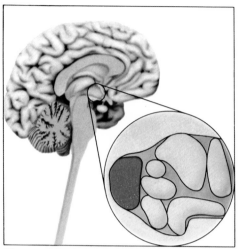

The sex drive is controlled by an area in the hypothalamus of the brain. This site, shown here in red, is called the posterior hypothalamic area.

Testosterone is produced in the testes of the male and in the adrenal glands of both sexes. Women, therefore, have about one-twentieth of the male amount. Since hormone levels alone do not determine the extent of sex drive in humans, female sexual capacity is comparable with that of the male, although women are more strongly influenced by convention and culture. Similarly, there is no very direct relationship between the amount of testosterone a man produces and his sex drive. Research has shown that once sexual activity is established as a source of enjoyment, its intrinsic rewards make it largely independent of hormonal status.

Stimulus response pathways in sex

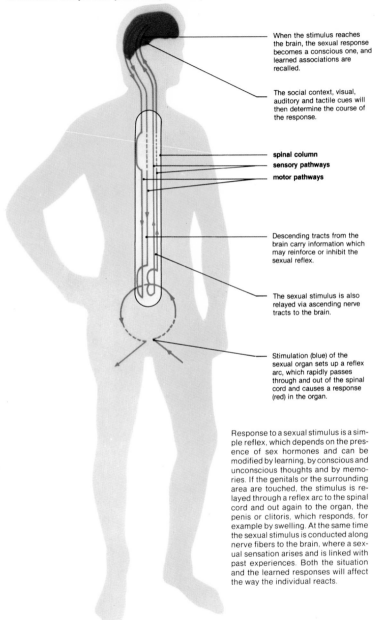

When the stimulus reaches the brain, the sexual response becomes a conscious one, and learned associations are recalled.

The social context, visual, auditory and tactile cues will then determine the course of the response.

spinal column
sensory pathways
motor pathways

Descending tracts from the brain carry information which may reinforce or inhibit the sexual reflex.

The sexual stimulus is also relayed via ascending nerve tracts to the brain.

Stimulation (blue) of the sexual organ sets up a reflex arc, which rapidly passes through and out of the spinal cord and causes a response (red) in the organ.

Response to a sexual stimulus is a simple reflex, which depends on the presence of sex hormones and can be modified by learning, by conscious and unconscious thoughts and by memories. If the genitals or the surrounding area are touched, the stimulus is relayed through a reflex arc to the spinal cord and out again to the organ, the penis or clitoris, which responds, for example by swelling. At the same time the sexual stimulus is conducted along nerve fibers to the brain, where a sexual sensation arises and is linked with past experiences. Both the situation and the learned responses will affect the way the individual reacts.

From: ATLAS OF THE BODY AND MIND. © Mitchell Beazley Publishers, Ltd. 1976. Published in U.S.A. by Rand McNally & Company.

The regulation of metabolism

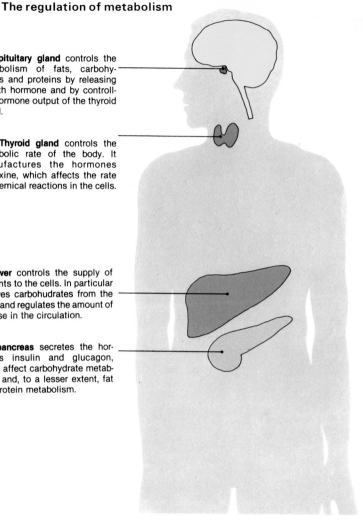

The pituitary gland controls the metabolism of fats, carbohydrates and proteins by releasing growth hormone and by controlling hormone output of the thyroid gland.

The Thyroid gland controls the metabolic rate of the body. It manufactures the hormones thyroxine, which affects the rate of chemical reactions in the cells.

The liver controls the supply of nutrients to the cells. In particular it sieves carbohudrates from the blood and regulates the amount of glucose in the circulation.

The pancreas secretes the hormones insulin and glucagon, which affect carbohydrate metabolism and, to a lesser extent, fat and protein metabolism.

The overall metabolism of the body is governed and constantly monitored by various organs of the body which are anatomically separate, but which function as a complete unit.

Metabolism involves chemical changes. The hypothalamus monitors and regulates the state of the body's metabolism and is a vital force in sexual drives.

From: ATLAS OF THE BODY AND MIND. © Mitchell Beazley Publishers, Ltd. 1976. Published in U.S.A. by Rand McNally & Company.

Male reproductive organs

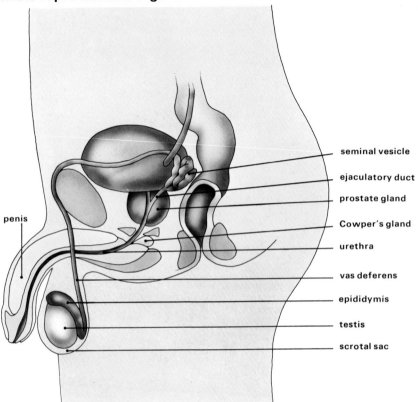

seminal vesicle

ejaculatory duct

prostate gland

Cowper's gland

urethra

vas deferens

epididymis

testis

scrotal sac

penis

The male sex organs, shown from the side and front, are essentially two glands, or testes, producing hormones and sperm, and a system of tubes which enable the sperm to be transferred to the female. The testes are contained in the scrotum hanging outside the pelvis. From puberty, each testis continually manufactures sperm which are transported to the epididymis, where they are stored until they mature, and then to the vas deferen. Cells in the testes also secrete the hormone testosterone, which controls development of the male sex organs and the secondary sex characteristics.

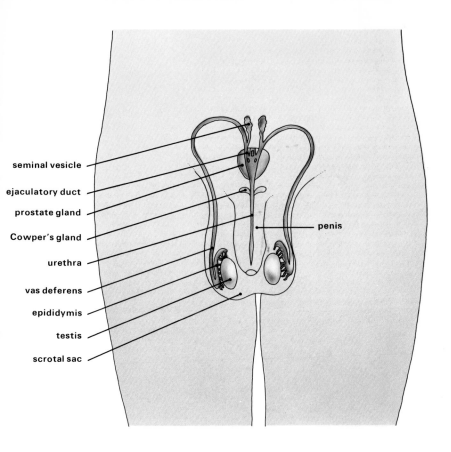

seminal vesicle

ejaculatory duct

prostate gland

Cowper's gland

urethra

vas deferens

epididymis

testis

scrotal sac

penis

The rhythmic contractions force sperm into the urethra, which is also the route for excretion of urine. The paired seminal vesicles secrete a sugary fluid just before the sperm reach the ejaculatory duct. The prostate gland adds a milky, alkaline fluid, and a pair of Cowper's glands contribute mucus. The semen, which is ejaculated through the penis, is a mixture of sperm and these fluids. One ejaculate may contain as many as one hundred million sperm.

From: ATLAS OF THE BODY AND MIND. © Mitchell Beazley Publishers, Ltd. 1976. Published in U.S.A. by Rand McNally & Company.

Female reproductive organs

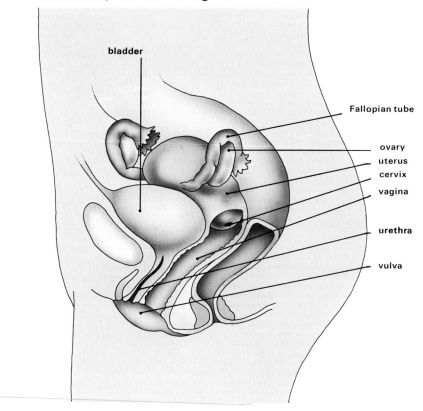

bladder

Fallopian tube

ovary
uterus
cervix

vagina

urethra

vulva

The female sex organs, shown from the side and the front, lie in the lower abdomen, where they are protected by the bony pelvis. At puberty, the two almond-shaped ovaries begin to produce the female hormones, estrogen and progesterone, and the sex cells, or ova. Each month, the ovary releases an ovum into the funnel-shaped opening of a Fallopian tube. If coitus occurs it is here that the ovum may be fertilized. Each Fallopian tube is approximately four inches long and is lined with ciliated cells.

From: ATLAS OF THE BODY AND MIND. © Mitchell Beazley Publishers, Ltd. 1976. Published in U.S.A. by Rand McNally & Company.

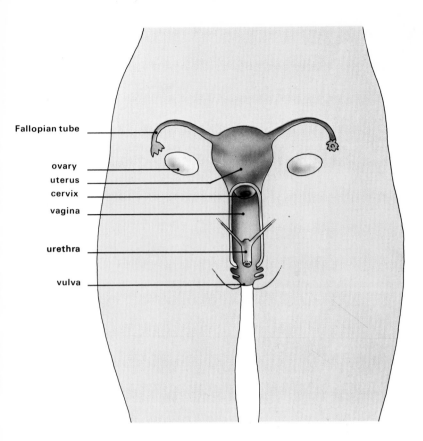

Fallopian tube

ovary
uterus
cervix
vagina

urethra

vulva

The two Fallopian tubes lead into the womb, or uterus, a three-inch-long pear-shaped organ lined with the endometrium, which is shed and built up again each month. It is in this endometrium that the fertilized egg implants and grows during pregnancy. The neck of the womb, or cervix, joins the uterus with the muscular vagina, which leads to the external genitalia, or vulva. The female urinary system, unlike that of the male, is separate from the reproductive system. The bladder empties into the urethra, which opens just in front of the vagina.

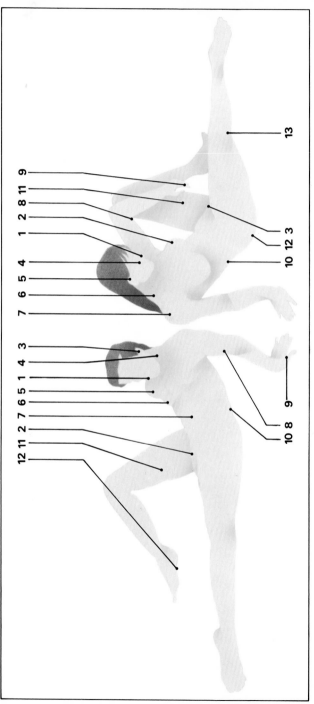

The areas of the body where contact is particularly effective in arousing sexual feelings are known as erogenous zones. Although there are variations between men and women and in individuals, the main **female** erogenous zones are the lips, the inside of the mouth and the tongue (1), the breasts and nipples (2), and the genitals (3). Also sensitive are the cheeks (4), the ears (5), the neck (6), the shoulders (7), the insides of the arms (8), the hands (9), the waist (10), the insides of the thighs (11), the buttocks (12), and the backs of the knees (13).

The **male** erogenous zones include the lips, the inside of the mouth and the tongue (1), the genitals (2), the ears (3), the neck (4), the shoulders (5), the nipples (6), the navel (7), the insides of the arms (8), the hands (9), the base of the spine (10), the insides of the thighs (11) and the soles of the feet (12).

Initially the wife will endure the act of sexual intercourse hoping her husband will ejaculate quickly. Soon her being used as a mechanical container may be frustrating to the point of resentment. To avoid sex, they may complain of a headache or try to distract the husband by discussing financial problems or other problems at home.

Men react to this frigidity in their wives in various ways. Some may accept it while other men may have feelings of rejection.

Achieving Proper Function

To correct this condition, the wife must be relaxed and free of emotional disturbances. This is necessary for the involuntary smooth muscles that control sexual arousal to function as they should. A wife who is suddenly faced with her husband's preliminary actions prior to intercourse must not be upset or have negative emotions.

If she is, there will be a hypersecretion of acid which not only upsets her digestive system but also charges the smooth muscles which go into a spasm. As a result, the genital swelling subsides, the lubrication of her vagina stops and the vaginal channel reduces to its pre-intercourse smaller size. She will fail to respond sexually.

Communication Vital

Again lack of communication between husband and wife as to their sexual needs, preferences or problems can be the root cause that triggers frigidity. She may have an anticipatory fear that she will not reach orgasm. Or there may be a special sexual approach that she likes but is afraid to ask her husband to perform.

As an example, the wife may secretly desire _cunnilingus_[1] but her husband may be turned off at the mere suggestion. She accommodates his desires but eventually she tends to frigidity because she is not satisfied sexually. It can also work the other way. The husband may prefer _fellatio_[2] but such an act may be repulsive to the wife.

Treatment Approaches

Pressure For Performance Removed

Initial treatment for general sexual dysfunction in the female is to forego sexual intercourse and orgasm for a period of time. In this way there is no pressure put on her to perform sexually. Instead, the wife caresses her husband and their erotic activity is one of gently touching. The wife takes the initiative and when the moment is appropriate the husband returns the caresses. This period of erotic activity without her husband seeking intercourse generates an atmosphere conducive to making the wife more self-assured.

[1]Cunnilingus _is sexual activity in which the husband's mouth and tongue are used to stimulate his wife's genitalia including the clitoris._

[2]Fellatio _is insertion of the penis into the mouth for purposes of sexual gratification._

**Patience
Needed**

The husband should not become impatient nor clumsy in returning caresses with his wife. Nor should he at this initial period touch her erotic areas. It should be a time of relaxation for both husband and wife without a demand performance for intercourse.

Masters and Johnson, well-known therapists, suggest that after this first approach has been successfully completed, the couple should then proceed to the teasing genital play stage.

**Guidance
By Wife
Needed**

In this next step to reduce female sexual dysfunction, the husband gently and teasingly touches his wife's nipples, her vagina entrance and her clitoral area. This touching should not stimulate an orgasm. If the wife is dry, he should apply vaseline or other lubricant to her vaginal area. The wife should advise her husband what areas give her the most pulsating satisfaction.

This will take patience and time and may be frustrating for the husband. If this sexual stimulation requires it, the wife should bring her husband to an ejaculation either manually or orally . . . but not vaginally.

After the first two steps have been successfully accomplished (and this may take several weeks), the couple is ready to proceed with the third step which is actual sexual intercourse.

There must be no pressure or demand from the husband. Again the husband will teas-

Only through mutual understanding, patience and love can sexual problems between husband and wife be solved.

ingly touch his wife's most erotic sensitive areas and gently stimulate her clitoris until the time he can feel the flow of lubrication in her vagina.

Wife Initiates Act

Dr. Helen Singer Kaplan, in her book, The New Sex Therapy, suggests that at this point of arousal, it is important that the *female* initiates sexual intercourse *(coitus).* The husband should thrust slowly, not in a fast, demanding way. The wife should concentrate on the action enjoying the physical sensations she experiences in her vagina as her husband's erect penis *(phallus)* moves against the vaginal wall and clitoris.

The wife should employ coital thrusting and contract her pubic muscles. If the husband approaches ejaculation too quickly, the couple should separate until the intensity subsides. This repeated on-off procedure is often very arousing to the female . . . because no performance is expected. If the wife does not complete an orgasm, she should finally bring her husband to an ejaculatory response.

Speed Is Not The Key!

In this impatient society, we are so used to Minute Rice, instant mashed patatoes, quickee car washes and instant coffee that we tend to think every other problem including sexual problems should be resolved instantly. But we are not dealing with machines, we are dealing with responsive human beings who are emotionally complex in their structure.

Patience, they say, is a virtue seldom found in woman . . . *but never found in man!*

So when a husband finds his 3-step approach to his wife's frigidity did not work according to plan . . . he is prone to give up. He must realize that disagreements are not disasters but rather a sign of progress. If these *"disasters"* are vocalized between husband and wife in honest communications . . . these inborn fears can become firm foundations on which to build mutual trust and respect.

Once this hurdle is crossed, it is quite possible husband and wife will experience the most fulfilling sexual life ever!

Hidden Worries

It is not uncommon during this 3-step approach for the woman to express common fears which she may not vocalize to her husband. Dr. Kaplan reports on some of these fears:

> She thinks,
> *Is he getting tired?*
> *He must think I'm really neurotic*
> *This is not what he wants to do.*
> *I can't ask him to service me like this.*
> *I'm sure he wishes he were with*
> *a more responsive woman.*[1]

Sometimes there are deep underlying root causes for general sexual dysfunction. And initially, the 3-step renewal approach may appear successful but suddenly blow up into an argument or renewed frigidity.

---

[1]Helen Singer Kaplan, M.D., Ph.D., The New Sex Therapy (New York: Times Books) 1974, p. 370.

Understanding Essential

Honest communication could uncover a common barrier some women may have towards marriage. Marriage can be thought of by her as a form of bondage. The wife became married, in part perhaps, to be assured of financial security. But in turn for this financial security she finds herself having to *"service"* her husband's sexual needs, live in submission to his every whim and deny herself certain creative goals.

Understanding this, the husband can play an important part in removing these hidden fears from his wife. And this is the first step to correcting his wife's frigidity.

19

THE FEMALE AND ORGASMS

Orgasmic Dysfunction Problems

Orgastic (or Orgasmic) dysfunction is another common complaint of women. There are various classifications of this problem.

Primary Orgasmic Dysfunction is a condition where the woman has never experienced an orgasm.

Secondary Orgasmic Dysfunction is a condition where the woman who was regularly orgasmic and did have climaxes can no longer experience an orgasm.

Coital Orgasmic Inadequacy is a condition where a woman cannot achieve an orgasm during sexual intercourse but can achieve an orgasm through other stimulation. This is sometimes called a *situational* dysfunction.

Absolute Orgasmic Dysfunction is a condition where the woman is unable to achieve either a clitoral-induced or sexual intercourse-induced orgasm under any circumstance.

Lubricates Copiously

The frustrating part of this female sexual problem is that these women may have a very strong sex drive. During sexual foreplay they will lubricate copiously. The wife may exhibit erotic sensations as her husband's penis penetrates her vagina. While she should be sufficiently aroused to have an orgasm . . . nothing happens!

Orgasms

There have been many discussions among sex therapists as to whether there are two types of orgasm in the female ... the clitoral orgasm and the vaginal orgasm.

Vulval Orgasm

To this has been added the vulval orgasm which is described as involuntary rhythmic contractions of muscles in the walls of the vulva. This starts in the outer third of the vagina and spreads upward to the uterus. This may bring muscular contractions in the buttocks and legs.

Uterine Orgasm

Another suggested orgasm is uterine orgasm which comes about when the penis bounces against the wall of the cervix at the back of the vagina. This brings a special feeling to the abdomen and muscles of the diaphragm and throat.

Don't Dwell On Mechanics

There is a danger that the husband and wife become too concerned with the mechanics of orgasm. Guilt, hostility, insecurity can come from a wife who feels she is not responding according to her husband's expectations. Or he may tend towards impotency because he feels he is unable to "push the right button" to release her into multiple orgasms.

One Type Female Orgasm

Those who have made a study of the subject (in recent years) seem to agree that there is only one kind of female orgasm. It is an orgasm that initially is triggered by clitoral stimulation which then spreads to the entire vaginal area. Both the clitoris and vagina become part of the female orgasm.

The clitoris is a vital link to restoring or starting an orgasm in the female. Vaginal stimulation is important and pleasurable but it will not trigger orgasm.

The degree of stimulation given to the clitoris will determine the intensity of orgasm. To achieve the most intense physical stimulation, direct manipulation of the clitoris by the hand or mouth is indicated.

Female Superior Position

Actual sexual intercourse provides only a mild clitoral stimulation. Of the various positions for sexual intercourse, the female superior position is the best position to provide good stimulation of the clitoris.

Then, too, the amount of stimulation necessary to achieve female orgasm can vary in the same woman under different circumstances. At one time the woman can achieve orgasm after two or three thrusts by her husband. Yet, on other occasions, two or three minutes (or more) of thrusting may be necessary to bring orgasm.

Unsatisfactory Approach

Some husbands, so concerned with their own desire to quickly release their ejaculation, never bring their wife to an orgasm via sexual intercourse. Instead they manually manipulate the clitoris until orgasm comes. Generally, the wife finds this highly unsatisfactory because it conveys the impression that her husband is merely accommodating her and being sexually selfish.

It is estimated that some 10% of wives never achieve an orgasm of any kind. Some females only achieve orgasm after lengthy clitoral stimulation. Others can only achieve it by manual or oral stimulation . . . while still others, only by use of a vibrator.

Orgasmic Platform

The 8/10ths of a second pulsating spasms are quickly spent by the male when he ejaculates. But the orgasm in the female reaches a pleasurable plateau and may not be fully lost for 20 or 30 minutes. This period of time is sometimes called the *orgasmic platform.*

Anxiety . . . A Contributing Cause

Hidden Fears Hinder Response

Anxiety has long been recognized as a contributing cause of orgasmic dysfunction in women as well as in men. The man who measures his own virility against the orgasmic responses of his wife may be contributing to her inability to have an orgasm.

Then, too, some women actually fear if they allow themselves to have an orgasm they will urinate or become convulsive. In some cases, depression makes a woman inadequate to have orgasm. Boredom, monotony or hostility can also be factors. And some women are actually sexually ignorant, not realizing what sexual activity will arouse them.

Initially, the therapy approach to this problem is to encourage the woman to release her involuntary *"over-control"* of the re-flexes that bring orgasm.

Treatment For Primary Orgasmic Dysfunction

Clitoral Stimulation Therapy

A woman who has never achieved orgasm *(Primary Orgasmic Dysfunction)* is encour-aged by the therapist to manipulate her clitoris to the level of erotic excitement. At this point, many stop because they feel un-comfortable. After several attempts, the woman is encouraged to continue even though uncomfortable until orgasm is achieved. Sometimes a vibrator is used to achieve clitoral stimulation. The vibrator is only used once or twice as this does not resemble the normal sensations found dur-ing intercourse.

During intercourse the woman is in-structed to thrust actively with her hus-band and contract her vaginal and ab-dominal muscles when she feels the sensa-tion of impending orgasm. She should not seek to *"perform"* for her husband but rather, to relax mentally. If she becomes concerned over whether she will climax or not, she will short-circuit the action of her involuntary muscles. After her husband has ejaculated (and if she has not had an orgasm), he should then fondle her clitoris leisurely until orgasm comes.

Too often the wife subdues her sexual needs in order to satisfy her husband's needs. Upon seeing her husband's erect penis, she unconsciously feels she must take care of him at once. And quite selfishly, he seeks quick sexual release. Once he has ejaculated, he rapidly loses interest in sex and may fall asleep . . . leaving his wife in a state of unfulfilled arousal. This continual frustration leads to problems.

Coital Orgasmic Inadequcy

Leisurely Foreplay Essential

Coital Orgasmic Inadequacy is a type of frigidity where the woman cannot achieve orgasm within the format of sexual intercourse. She most likely will enjoy the intimacy of sexual intercourse with the penis in her vagina but the act does not sufficiently stimulate her clitoris to bring about an orgasm or climax.

The husband, to help correct this problem should take the time to heighten his wife's sexual arousal prior to penis-penetration of her vagina. This foreplay, if done properly, will bring her to a state of high sexual arousal lowering her orgasm threshold prior to entry. The thrusting provided by coitus should then trigger orgasm.

Part of the foreplay can be a teasing technique where the wife is highly aroused, the husband inserts his penis into the vagina. and slowly beings thrusting. In a short time, he withdraws and repeats the procedure. This "start-stop" technique can be highly effective in bringing arousal in the wife.

FEMALE SEX ORGANS

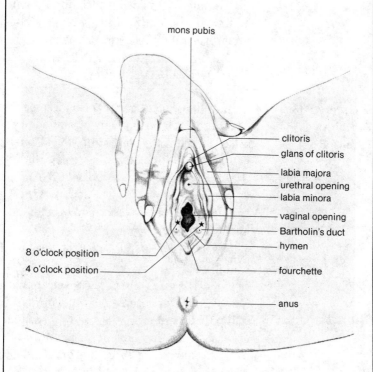

mons pubis

clitoris

glans of clitoris

labia majora

urethral opening

labia minora

vaginal opening

Bartholin's duct

hymen

8 o'clock position

4 o'clock position

fourchette

anus

The labia minora are the *"lips of the vulva."* This is the area that changes to a deep red as the woman reaches the orgasm plateau.

The <u>outer</u> third of the vaginal skin is a sensitive area. Particularly sensitive, beside the clitoris, is the 4 o'clock and 8 o'clock positions noted in the illustration above.

Art adapted from various medical drawings by Bob Jackson.

Variations of this technique include the husband thrusting to the point of impending ejaculation. He stops and without withdrawing, stimulates his wife's clitoris stopping just short of her orgasm. Then the thrusting begins again vigorously to achieve mutual orgasm.

Two Sensitive Areas

The husband should also strive to arouse his wife to vaginal erotic sensations. The vagina has two sensitive areas:

1. The outer third of the vaginal skin. (The inner two-thirds of the vagina are insensitive and unresponsive to touch.)

   Some women have pleasurable erotic sensations when penetrating pressure is applied to the outer vaginal area either at the 4 or 8 o'clock position.

2. The adjacent *labia minora* are the "lips of the vulva" and have been termed the *"sex skin."* They are the lips that enclose the clitoris. This is called the *"sex skin"* because as the woman reaches the orgasm plateau vivid color changes occur. The skin changes from a pink to a bright red, even to a deep purple. The more brilliant the color change, the more intense the wife's response to that particular form of sexual stimulation. After orgasm, the skin changes to a light pink within 10-15 seconds.

Wife Controls Response

Another technique to bring about the wife's orgasm during intercourse is for the husband to manually stimulate his wife's clitoris to a point near orgasm while his erect penis is in her vagina. This is done in the female superior position. In this particular variation, the husband lies on his back. His wife sits astride him, facing him, in a kneeling position and lowers herself on to his erect penis.

When the husband's stimulation of her clitoris reaches a point of impending orgasm, she signals him to stop. At this point, the wife begins to thrust actively to achieve mutual orgasm. Because she is in the female superior position, she can manipulate her thrusting action against the erect penis so the most sensitive vaginal and clitoral areas are aroused.

High Arousal Possible

In some situations where these approaches fail to bring orgasm in a woman, self stimulation during intercourse may prove successful. In this technique the wife is on her back with the husband on his side. One leg is between her husband's leg. Her other leg is over her husband resting over his buttocks. He enters from a rear-side position. This gives her opportunity to stimulate her clitoris while having intercourse. She stops stimulating herself when near orgasm and joins in mutual climax by thrusting. This technique can bring high arousal in both husband and wife.

20

THE FEMALE AND FEAR OF INTERCOURSE

Vaginal Entrance Closes

Vaginismus is a conditioned spasm of the muscle surrounding the vaginal entrance. This muscle snaps shuts so tightly whenever penetration is attempted that sexual intercourse may become impossible.

Surprisingly, vaginismus is a common cause of unconsummated marriages. This condition can last many years ... yet it is one of the dysfunctions most successfully treated.

Because the woman has a fear of intercourse and penis penetration, any attempt at intercourse is painful. The wife may be sexually responsive but the moment coitus is attempted, her vagina snaps shut. They continue to enjoy sexual foreplay, clitoral stimulation and other erotic arousals as long as it does not lead to sexual intercourse.

EPISIOTOMY

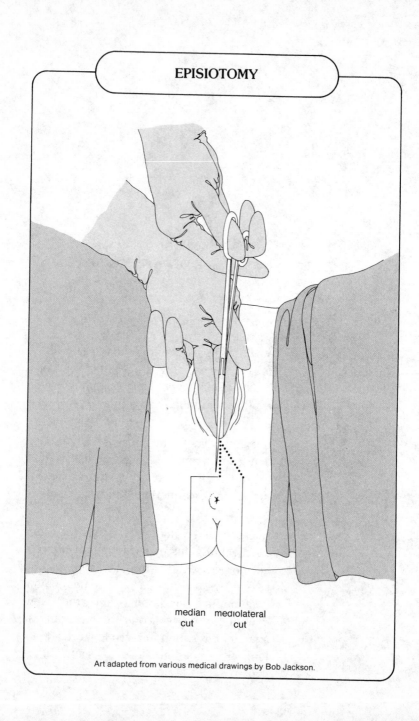

median   mediolateral
cut   cut

Art adapted from various medical drawings by Bob Jackson.

**Lubrication
Present**

Oddly enough, vaginal lubrication is present in these women during sexual arousal and they, themselves, become distressed by their inability to participate pleasurably with their husband in sexual intercourse.

Not understanding the problem, both husband and wife can drift towards impotence and frigidity if the problem is not resolved. The wife may want help but is frightened that the cure will be worse than the disease. Her husband's repeated attempts to penetrate her cause only more pain and humiliation and leads to frustration for both parties. Her husband may seek other avenues for his sexual gratification. And this fear of rejection and abandonment may further aggravate her dilemma. Because these are involuntary muscles, any mental block or emotional disturbance will heighten the problem.

Physical Causes of Vaginismus

**Episiotomy
May Cause
Problem**

Often when a women delivers a baby, an *episiotomy* is performed by the doctor. An episiotomy is a scissors incision made in the skin below the vaginal opening as the baby is about to emerge. The incision is made to prevent tearing during the delivery and to speed delivery. After delivery, the incision is sutured and the stitches dissolve in a few days. Aftereffects may include a burning and aching at the site of incision. Sexual relations are delayed and the scar remains as numb area in the tissues.

Episiotomy is performed in about 90% of all hospital deliveries in the United States. With doctors in European hospitals, however, only about 12% perform episiotomy. There is much disagreement on the merits of episiotomy.

Delivery Table Not Best For Mother

The very position the mother is in on the delivery table in U.S. hospitals is a cause of debate. It is convenient for the doctor but not deemed by many to be the best method of delivering a baby. The mother lies on her back. Her legs are held apart in stirrups which encourage over-stretching and tearing of the skin more likely. In Europe, in many cases, no leg restraints are used nor stirrups. The obstetricians there are trained to support and massage the intact perineum during delivery . . . thus assisting the dilation of the skin without tearing.

A Questionable Benefit

In the United States, many physicians believe that episiotomy preserves the tone of the pelvic floor muscles. However, European doctors, where no episiotomy is performed, report no higher incidence of weak pelvic floor muscles.

A poorly healed episiotomy can trigger vaginismus in a woman. Her recollection of pain and discomfort from this procedure may subsconsciously cause her involuntary vaginal muscles to close whenever penetration is attempted. She may also have suffered from obstetric trauma. The forceps used to complete delivery may have conveyed discomfort or fear.

Hymen Abnormalities May Contribute To Problem

Hymen abnormalities could also contribute to vaginismus. The hymen *is a membrane of tissue that covers and partly closes the opening of the vagina.* The hymen usually has a rather small opening before a girl has initial sexual intercourse. The opening will accept tampons. Contrary to old wives tales, most young women do not bleed at first intercourse. The hymen is not that tight that it will not accommodate the penis.

Imperforate Hymen

However, in some young women, the hymen opening is smaller than usual and pain and bleeding can occur when penetration is attempted. Some women also have a hymen that has no opening. This is called an *imperforate hymen.* If this is present, the teenage girl will have a menstrual flow that cannot be discharged and thus no periods. This condition exists in about one out of 2000 women. This trapped blood after several months will cause obvious discomfort. A minor operation is done at the hospital to make an opening in the hymen. Any girl who cannot insert a tampon should consult a physician to check the structure of the hymen.

Cribriform Hymen

Cribriform hymen is a condition where the hymen has several small perforations instead of a single opening. These small perforations will allow drainage of menstrual flow but they will not allow penetration of a penis.

Such conditions can trigger the involuntary vaginal muscles into vaginismus.

Emotional Causes of Vaginismus

**Non-Biblical
Attitudes
Can Cause
Vaginismus**

One need only read Genesis 2:23-25, 4:1 or the Song of Solomon or Proverbs 5:15-21 in the Old Testament or Matthew 19:5, 1 Timothy 2:15; 5:14 in the New Testament to realize that sexual intercourse within the confines of marriage is ordained of God.

Many women (and men) who are brought up in an atmosphere of a strict religious background, subconsciously perhaps, develop a warped attitude of sex. As youngsters they feel very restricted and may associate all sexual desires as evil. In the area of sex, their parents may be non-communicative.

Their parents may also harbor sexual misconceptions. Although they may be very orthodox Biblically, they may have traditional but non-Biblical attitudes on what constitutes a wholesome sexual experience. "*Traditional*" is meant in the sense that wrong religious orthodoxy would convey that sexual intercourse is not for pleasure but should only be employed when a child is desired. It should only be a duty . . . not a delight! Some cults also adopt this attitude towards sex.

**Subconscious
Triggers
Response**

One can see that such upbringing may have a tendency to make a husband impotent and a wife, frigid. In the woman, she may develop or enter marriage with vaginismus . . . wanting sexual arousal and response but unable to deliver. The sight of her husband's penis approaching her vagina triggers the vaginal muscles to snap shut to avoid penetration.

There are other factors that can cause emotionally-induced vaginismus. It may come as a consequence of a childhood or adolescent experience where she was raped. Perhaps as a child she was sexually molested by some member in her family or a close friend of the family.

Incest
A Growing
Problem

Incest could also be a contributing factor. Incest is defined as sexual relations between parent and child or between brother and sister. Incest in our society is far more common than was once believed.

Studies indicate there are about 360,000 cases of childhood sexual abuse a year, roughly 38% of them incest. Among these cases, we do not know the incidence of forced or violent incest, but it must be extremely high; otherwise the acts would not have made the grade of becoming a statistic. Quiet, hidden incest probably does not get reported very often. . . . Children get involved in incest because it's urged on them and they do not know that it is not acceptable.[1]

Vaginismus can occur because of a number of complex reasons from the range of organic to emotional deep seated fears of penis penetration.

---

[1]Avodah K. Offit, M.D., Night Thoughts, Reflections of a Sex Therapist, (New York: Congdon & Lattes, Inc.) 1981, pp. 184, 185.

Treatment of Vaginismus

Re-educating Involuntary Response

Initially treatment is centered around educating the woman what is occurring during this involuntary constriction of her vagina. A pelvic examination is done by a doctor who understands the problem and proceeds slowly, explaining each move to his patient. He shows her the vaginal speculum he will use in an attempt to examine her vagina. He places supports under her knees rather than placing her legs in restrictive stirrups.

In the second examination session, the husband is urged to be present . . . so that the nature of the involuntary constriction about the vagina can be demonstrated to both partners. The woman is encouraged to watch the examination in a mirror held by a medical assistant.[1]

Dilators Aid Therapy

At this point, the gynecologist gently inserts graduated dilators into the vagina. The first dilator is very slender. The width and length of the dilators begin at the narrow-small size and graduate to a width and length the size of an erect penis. As treatment progresses, the various larger sizes are introduced into the vagina. The final size may not be inserted until 5-10 dilation sessions.

---

[1]Robert C. Kolodny, William H. Masters, Virginia E. Johnson, Textbook of Sexual Medicine (Boston: Little, Brown and Company) 1979, p. 539.

The purpose of the dilators is to reprogram the muscular contractions. The woman is told to tighten her pelvic muscles as intensely as she can. She is told to hold this tightness for about 4 seconds, then let go. This deliberate tightening is designed to overcome the involuntary tightening of her vaginal muscles. It is after this "tensing and letting go" cycle for a few minutes that the initial smallest size dilator is presented to her.

Controlling Muscle Response

Before inserting the small dilator, the physician inserts a well-lubricated gloved finger at the opening of her vagina. The woman is asked to tighten the vaginal muscles and then to release them. At the point of relaxation, the physician inserts the finger into the vagina as the woman watches the procedure in the mirror.

After success in this procedure, the smallest dilator is inserted very slowly. She is then asked to reach down and touch the base of the dilator and move it gently. Often, she is surprised that the entire dilator is actually within her vagina.

Then she is told to remove and insert the dilator herself and to repeat this procedure several times.

The woman is asked to take the dilator home and to practice insertion at least 4 times a day, making sure it is lubricated, leaving it in 15 minutes each time.

**Remains
All
Night**

She is also asked to insert the dilator before she goes to bed at night and to leave it in all night. Dilator sizes start at the smallest size, No. 1 and progress to the erect penis size, No. 5. Most women can progress from No. 1 size to No. 4 size within a period of one week. The dilators are made of inflexible plastic or rubber. Some are made of glass.

To women with an aversion to dilators, the wife is encouraged to insert her own finger .. or the husband uses his fingers for her therapy. In some cases, the woman will use a tampon because she is familiar with this.

After success with No. 4, the wife is asked to proceed with intercourse with her husband. So she has freedom of movement, the female superior position is recommended. To erase any fears of failure, the woman is told she can apply an artificial lubricant to her husband's penis before lowering her vagina into the position of penile penetration.

To help her shed her phobia (fear) of penetration, she is encouraged to fantasize sexual situations in which her husband's penis plunges into her vagina.

**Slow
And
Gentle**

Initially in sexual intercourse, the husband's thrusting should be slow and gentle. He should withdraw immediately if his wife requests it. Although she may find this initial intercourse "unpleasant," she is encouraged to continue with it to overcome the negative involuntary muscle signals that cause vaginismus. By so doing, sexual intercourse becomes a highly pleasurable experience.

Many times, vaginismus in marriage occurs because of earlier negative sexual experiences in one's younger years. Thus, any time the wife's husband attempts penetration of his penis into her vagina, she automatically develops an avoidance reaction and her vaginal muscles snap shut involuntarily.

Hidden Fears

Many women who have had vaginismus will relate that even in therapy they have an inborn fear that the unpleasant feelings initially of penile penetration may increase. Once this fear is surmounted, the problem can be resolved within two to six weeks.

Surgery Not The Answer

If the problem is not resolved, the couple will be unable to have intercourse or to have children. Surgically, the problem can be resolved by an operation called a *perineotomy*. In the female the perineum is the external region between the vulva and the anus. It is this muscle area that is surgically corrected.

Such an operation is not entirely satisfactory. It will enable the couple to have intercourse. However, most women who are sexually responsive prior to surgery (although unable to accept the penis) lose their sexual arousal after surgery. Before surgery they enjoyed clitoral stimulation and were able to have multiple orgasms but after surgery, lose interest. The operation (which may necessitate up to 75 stitches) can be an emotional blow to the wife.

Vaginismus in most cases can be treated successfully. In other cases there are other underlying emotional problems. And when the wife suddenly becomes able to accept her husband's penis, he may find himself impotent and unable to function.

Sexual Anesthesia

A Lack Of Feeling

This does not refer to any operation . . . rather to the feeling some women have towards sex. Actually, it is their lack of feeling or interest that is the problem. They have become "*anesthesized*" or insensitive feeling <u>nothing</u> when sexually stimulated.

They may enjoy the closeness of physical contact but clitoral stimulation does not bring any response. They are so insensitive that they hardly know when the penis enters their vagina.

Rather than being a sexual dysfunction, it is an emotional problem with neurotic overtones. The wife may be trying to please her husband but her subconscious (through some previous negative experience) makes her normal sensitive areas insensitive to sexual arousal.

Treatment is aimed at finding the root causes for this behavior before mutually satisfactory intercourse can be resumed.

21

SEX AFTER 40 . . . OR 50 OR 60

**Greater
Fulfillment
Possible**

For some, life can begin at 40. For others it can begin to decline at 40. Apart from health, much has to do with one's mental and emotional attitudes towards life, towards one another, and most important, towards God.

Life is not always a mountaintop experience. If it were, perhaps we would not enjoy it as much for we would have nothing for comparison. Life has its valleys . . . sometimes deep valleys. And how refreshing that mountaintop experience comes after a time in a valley of despair or discouragement.

Marital sex after 40 or 50 or 60 or even 70 can be as fulfilling and satisfying (perhaps more satisfying) than at 20 or 30. It is important to have a happy, joyful attitude towards life. No, you don't have to walk around with a perpetual grin on your face. And if you just lost your job, you are not expected to come bouding into your home exclaiming to your wife, *"Praise the Lord . . . I lost my job!"*

**A Joyful
Inner
Spirit**

But your inner spirit should be one of peace and joy. If you have it, it will reflect in your outer disposition . . . even during trials and testings.

The Bible says in the Old Testament:

> *A merry (joyful) heart
> doeth good like a medicine:
> but a broken spirit
> drieth the bones.*
>
> (Proverbs 17:22)

As one gets older, sexual pleasure can be better than ever. It can be the cement that binds the couple to greater love and devotion to each other.

**Menopause
Emotions**

If there is not sexual harmony, these can be dangerous years for the married couple. The woman may seek a younger or more virile man to satisfy her increased sexuality . . . now that she has no fear of becoming pregnant. The man who suddenly realizes he is getting old may seek a younger companion to bolster his *"menopause"* emotions.

It is often after 40 that a woman's body is more vibrant, more responsive to her husband's caress. She is swifter to climax than she was at age 20. Usually, however, the male's sexual drive peaks in his late teens and the urgency and ability to climax takes longer after 40.

The Aging Man

Understanding Life's Changes

While there is no real reason for it, the number of sexually impotent men rises steadily with age. In his youth, the male has a high sex drive. He can achieve four to eight orgasms per day. Erection is instantaneous and he may maintain his erection for half an hour after ejaculating. His orgasm[1] experience is both intense and quick. And his ejaculation spurts forcefully 5 to 10 inches.

As men reach 30 sexual urgency diminishes. And by age 40 the frequency of orgasm changes significantly. The refractory period is also longer.[1]

As a man passes 60 and if he is not in top health the force of his ejaculatory stream may diminish and detumescence after orgasm is rapid.[2]

Reduction In Male Sex Hormone

As men get older there can be a gradual reduction in circulating levels of the male sex hormone, testosterone. Such changes can trigger depression, listlessness, poor

[1]Refractory period *is the time interval after ejaculation, when the male is physiologically unable to ejaculate again. In youth it may be as short as a few minutes. After 50 it may be as long as 12 to 24 hours.*

[2]Detumescence *is the subsiding of the erectile tissue of genital organs* (penis and clitoris) *following erection.*

appetite. It can also bring a decreased interest in sex even to the point of impotency. The male may easily tire and be irritable. With testosterone replacement therapy, these symptoms can be reversed over a 2-month period. If it is not, it can be an indication of some other physical ailment. The prostate gland may be diseased causing adverse sexual reactions.[1]

Then, too, with some older men, sexual activity can be satisfying without ejaculating at each intercourse opportunity.

In studies made with 261 men, E. Pfeiffer and his coworkers discovered that men primarily attributed the stopping of sexual activities to themselves. Some 40% cited impotence as their problem. There were 17% who indicated they stopped sexual activities because of ill health and 14% simply lost an interest in sex. Most women gave as the reason for stopping intercourse their husband's illness or marital problems.

Loss Of Sexual Interest

In this same study with both men and women aged 61 to 71, about 37% had intercourse at least once a week. In the age bracket of 66 to 71, there were 50% of the women who stated they had no sexual interest . . . whereas only 10% of the men said they had lost sexual interest.[2]

[1]You may wish to order PROSTATE PROBLEMS by Salem Kirban. Send $6 (This includes postage) to: Salem Kirban, Inc., Kent Road, Huntingdon Valley, Pennsylvania 19006.

[2]E. Pfeiffer, A. Verwoerdt, G. C. Davis, Sexual Behavior in Middle Life (American Journal of Psychiatry) 1972, 128:1262-1267.

Blood Flow Alterations Diminish Sex Drive

Alterations in blood flow to the genital organs can depress sexual function. This can come due to vascular diseases and the toll of poor nutritional habits in earlier years.

Boredom is also an important reason for loss of sex drive as one reaches 60 and beyond. In the Textbook of Sexual Medicine, the authors write:

> The instances of sexual attrition
> due to atrophy from disuse
> (*"use it or lose it"*)
> are encountered frequently
> in the geriatric years.
>
> The aging woman who abstains
> from sexual intercourse
> experiences a greater degree
> of shrinkage
> in the size of her vagina
> than does a woman
> of the same age
> who has continued sexual activity.
>
> The male in a similar situation
> of prolonged abstention
> often finds that with an attempted
> return to sexual activity
> he is unable to have erections.[1]

A woman may have a diminished vaginal lubrication but this does not indicate a lack of sexual interest but rather hormonal changes.

---

[1]Robert C. Kolodny, M.D., William H. Master, M.D., Virginia E. Johnson, D.Sc. (Hon.), Textbook of Sexual Medicine (Boston: Little, Brown and Company) 1979, p. 112.

The Aging Woman

**Women
More
Responsive
After 40**

Generally, girls are slower to awaken to sexuality. And initial intercourse as a young bride may be disappointing. The sex drive of the young husband is so intense that, out of ignorance, he ignores the slower sexual needs of his wife. Many young people enter marriage without a background of sound sexual counselling. Thus, their initial years may be beset with some stormy encounters, a few tears and some misunderstandings. Then, too, these earlier experiences can trigger impotence in the husband or frigidity in the wife as time progresses.

In the early twenties, frequency of intercourse between husband and wife is anywhere from two to five times per week. Generally at this age, it is the husband who receives satisfaction, not the wife.

Women tend to reach their most responsive years, sexually, in their early 40's. It is at this time that most female extra-marital involvements occurs. It is in this age group that vaginal lubrication occurs quickly and multiple orgasms are frequent. Some therapists compare vaginal lubrication in the female as equivalent to male erection.

**Hormonal
Production
Diminishes**

How a wife responds to sex during her menopausal years depends both on her health and her compatibility with her husband. Because she no longer menstruates there is a drastic drop in the circulating estrogen and progesterone hormones.

Positive Outlook Essential

In some women this change of life may bring with it irritability and other emotional changes including depression and a lack of interest in sex. Again, this depends on the woman's health, her outlook on life as well as that of her husband's.

A woman who has a positive outlook and whose life is Biblically-based should radiate a continued joy. Her desire to her husband should increase, rather than diminish. If the husband suddenly feels insecure and his wife is constantly nagging, such a relationship will not stimulate a healthy sex arousal in later years.

If her husband's sexual interest diminishes, then his wife's sexual responsiveness may decline as well. Even over 65, women report they have erotic dreams. Vaginal lubrication occurs more slowly and orgasm contractions decline. At age 30 a woman may have 5-7 orgasm contractions but this may decline to 2-3 after 65. Elderly women can, however, have multiple orgasms.

Erection Problems Occur

An aging husband, during sexual arousal, may find himself unable to get or maintain an erection. He panics. During the next lovemaking session, he becomes so concerned about the mechanics of erection that he again fails. These two impotent episodes can make him feel inadequate and encourage continued impotency. This is called secondary impotence (later impairment in a man who was once normally potent).

Misunderstandings Develop

Such action can trigger a pandora's box of misunderstandings. The wife may tell herself: "He doesn't find me sexy anymore. He used to get an erection just watching me undress."

It is during middle age that both partners can be highly vulnerable. This is particularly true if they do not understand the changing sexual patterns and if they do not honestly communicate with each other.

Stresses Can Reduce Sex

Middle-aged men appear to have a greater loss of sex drive than women. In today's role reversals, this aspect of sexuality may change. Previously, the husband had the responsibility of providing food and shelter for the home. His striving for survival and success in earning a living can take its toll in middle years. The stresses instead of being channeled into strengths can dampen desires for sexual relations.

In today's society, where women are taking on roles traditionally held by men, they, too may become the victims of this stress-filled environment.

Illness Can Discourage Sex

Heart disease and prostate problems are the two most frequently mentioned illnesses men have that end marital sex. Men who have had a heart attack tend to look at sexual intercourse as a strenuous activity.

However, doctors usually prescribe far more strenuous activity following a heart attack. Sexual intercourse is about on the par with taking a brisk walk.

Regular Intercourse Preserves Vagina

Alice Lake in What Women Over 35 Should Know About Themselves, writes:

> Within a decade after menopause,
> loss of estrogen alters the vagina,
> making its walls thinner,
> less elastic,
> more sensitive to irritation.
>
> The best treatment
> for this development
> is not medication,
> but sex.
>
> Regular intercourse
> once or twice a week
> helps preserve
> the size and shape of the vagina
> and slow the deterioration
> in lubricating ability.
>
> There is also some evidence
> that regular sex
> may stimulate
> production of estrogen.[1]

When a woman reaches 60 she may notice a shrinking in her clitoris. Sensitivity is not lost, however.

Dr. William Goode, a Stanford University sociologist has stated:

> *The most important sex organ*
> *is the mind.*

[1]Alice Lake, Our Own Years: What Women Over 35 Should Know About Themselves (New York: CBS Publications) 1979.

Negative Thoughts Reduce Sex Drive

Mutual sexual enjoyment between husband and wife should not cease or diminish simply because they are getting older. If they _think_ it should, this negative mental imagery will trigger a negative physical response.

Sexual Response Patterns In Younger and Older WOMEN

	Younger Women	Older Women
Breasts	Nipple erection Flush prior to orgasm	Nipple erection Less flushing
Clitoris	Full erection and high degree of sensitivity	Partial erection with continued sensitivity
Vagina	Copious vaginal lubrication within a few seconds	Reduced vaginal lubrication can take up to 5 minutes
	Vaginal lips thickened with reddish-purple appearance	Vaginal lips thin with less color change
	Slow collapse of expanded vagina after intercourse	Rapid collapse of expanded vagina after intercourse
Orgasms	Five to six contractions during orgasm	One to three contractions during orgasm
Rectum	Rectal sphincter contractions with orgasm	Less contractions

Unlike the male, the female does not need a refractory or rest phase after she has achieved orgasm. Seconds after she has achieved orgasm, and while she is still in the swollen plateau state, the woman can be stimulated to another, and another, until she is physically exhausted and no longer wishes further stimulation.[1]

[1]Helen Singer Kaplan, M.D., Ph.D., The New Sex Therapy (New York: Times Books) 1974, p. 12.

1
The Sex Drive

The sex drive is controlled by an area in the *hypothalamus* in the brain. Hypothalamus is a Greek word derivative meaning *under chamber.* It is part of the endocrine system. It is connected by many nerve tracts with the brain and spinal cord and acts as the link between the endocrine system and the nervous system.

The hypothalamus functions automatically. It is divided into 7 areas. These areas control the basic drives — hunger, thirst and sex.

1. Posterior area controls sexual drives.
2. Anterior area control thirst and drive to find water.
3. Dorsal (back) area is considered the human *"pleasure center."*

Other areas act as the body thermostat, and *appestat.* The appestat controls the hunger drive. Another area controls aggressive behavior.

The hypothalamus is very small (smaller than a walnut) but plays a crucial role in the quality of life and has a direct effect on the master endocrine gland, the *pituitary.*

The sex drive is composed of 3 contributing factors:

1. The brain triggers sexual desire when certain parts of the brain are activated. The sexual response and pleasure centers of the hypothalamus can be triggered into action visually by erotic objects, by touch or by smell. Touching your wife's nipple on her breast may create a desire in her for sexual union. The perfume she wears may generate a sexual arousal in the husband.

2. Environmental factors are part of the complex emotional areas that bring human sexual desire. Soft lights, a quiet bedroom, a husband and wife alone. The sexual arousal is further enhanced if both husband and wife feel financially secure, and are in good health and there are no disturbing outside noises. Certainly, a desire for sex can be diminished if you find yourself unable to pay your bills, you are worried, you have a headache and your apartment is underneath a bowling alley.

2
The Sex Drive

3.   Learned or cultural factors also enter in to a desire for sexual union. Experience, reason and learning are all powerful influences on our sex drive. After initial intercourse, a wife seeing her husband's erect penis has a learning experience that penetration into her vagina will produce a pleasurable plateau of ecstasy.

Often a husband and wife who normally do not get along and disagree and quarrel frequently ... can set aside their differences while they mutually enjoy each other in sexual intercourse. Sexual desire is an appetite which is physically similar to hunger. In normal, healthy couples, it is a virile, urgent drive that occurs in fulfillment at regular intervals.

Men and women have varying biological and psychological clocks. Many men like to have sexual intercourse the first thing in the morning. Many women don't! This can become a point of conflict most often in the treatment of impotence. The male sex hormone, _testosterone_ is highest in the man in the morning. For the male, testosterone levels are 25% lower in the evening. The man's sex hormone is lowest in the spring. It increases in the summer and peaks in September.[1]

Healthy men have an average of three to five erections a night. This usually occurs during the sleep cycle known as REM. REM means _rapid eye movement._ Rapid eye movements generally occur when a person is dreaming. A man in his middle age spends about a quarter of his sleep-time in sexual excitement. In one study made on men in their early 50's, about 1¼ hours of sleep-time was spent in full erection and ½ hour in partial erection.

Women also have REM sleep patterns where their vaginal blood flow is altered. Not sufficient study has been made to determine to what extent during these patterns there is clitoral enlargement.

-----

[1]Avodah K. Offit. M.D.. Night Thoughts (New York: Congdon & Lattes. Inc.) 1981. pp.17, 18, 78.

3
The Sex Drive

While a man's sex drive is not conditioned on how well he is groomed, the husband must realize that most women are uneasy about making love until they have gone through their beauty routine.

Some doctors believe that the _pubococcygeal_ muscle is responsible for orgasm in a woman. The stronger this PC muscle, the better the orgasm. To strengthen this muscle which surrounds the vagina area . . .

1. Squeeze your vagina as though stopping a urinary stream. Do not use your hands to squeeze . . . but concentrate on controlling the PC muscle. By so doing you can actually stop urination in midstream.
2. At the same time as the squeezing exercise, you press your belly to your backside causing internal muscle contractions. You will feel this overall tightening in your genital area.

This exercise will enhance orgasms and encourage multiple orgasms in the female.

Some men have decline in the levels of the sex male hormone, testosterone, after age 40. Because of this decline they often need more stimulation to achieve an erection.

Smells _(Olfaction)_ are a contributory factor to the sex drive. Husband and wife can either be turned on or off by genital odors of the opposite sex. It is believed that sexual odors are released by the _prepuce_ in the male and female. The prepuce in the female is the fold of skin that covers the clitoris. In the male the prepuce area is around the head of the penis. This aroma can be a powerful stimulant to triggering sexual desire.

22

SOME MALE MISCONCEPTIONS

**Husband's
Understanding
Essential**

Some women have been taught since childhood that sexual pleasure is only for man
and that sex is only for the purpose of having children. The wife was not created to
service her husband.

All husbands should become familiar with
the book of Genesis in the Old Testament of
the Bible. God created woman because he
did not want man to be alone so He said:

> I will make him a help meet for him . . .
> And the Lord God
> caused a deep sleep to fall upon Adam,
> and he slept:
> and He took one of his ribs . . .
> And the rib,
> which the Lord God had taken from man,
> made He a woman . . .
>
> (Genesis 2:18,21,22)

From reading this Scripture the husband
should realize that

> Woman was created from man's rib . . .
> so she could walk by his <u>side</u>
> and <u>not</u>
> from his foot
> to be stepped upon!

**Not
Lordly
Rule**

Many men think their manliness is upheld by lordly rule over their wife. With singleness of purpose, they remember the verse in the New Testament which says:

> *Wives,
> submit yourselves
> unto your own husbands . . .
> for the husband
> is the head of the wife.*
>
> (Ephesians 5:22,23)

But somehow, they fail to read the succeeding verses which state that husbands should love their wives *even as they love their own bodies!*

**Seek
Sensitivity
In
Love**

If a husband, in his youth, fails to consider the feelings of his wife . . . if he fails to share with her, his plans and his innermost thoughts . . . chances are middle age will only heighten this lack of sensitivity.

Someone once said that

> *A husband is a man
> who expects his wife
> to be perfect
> and to understand why he isn't!*

One irate husband was once heard to remark to his wife:

> *Light bill, water bill, gas bill,
> milk bill—
> you've got to quit this wild spending!*

When a man and woman marry, they become one. Of course, they must decide which one! And that is often where the storm starts.

**Humility
Is
Strength**

Unless a husband and wife learn to combine their best qualities as one and recognize their faults . . . middle age can lead to a rapid change in their sexuality. Too often a husband fails to exercise humility. Humility leads to strength and not to weakness.

**Macho
Image
Is
Weakness**

A husband who through his entire life tries to convey a <u>macho</u> image is really demonstrating his immaturity and insecurity. He may treat his wife as a slave who should answer his every beck and call. It is easy to understand why a wife sighs in relief when the affects of aging slow him down sexually to a mere whimper.

On the other hand, if the marriage has been one of sweet communion and gentle, loving sexual relations based on mutual trust, understanding and love . . . the sex life in later years should prove highly rewarding and stimulating.

In a healthy marriage, the desire for loving, for caressing, for sexual union exists until we die. If those in their 60's find sexual intercourse *"an overrated activity"* it is because either one or both partners have an organic or emotional problem.

In a healthy marriage, the spurts of impulsive sexual <u>intensity</u> that were prevalent in one's younger years should even out to a <u>higher sustained plateau</u> of sexual joy in the mellow years of life.

23

UNDERSTANDING MALE SEXUAL RESPONSE

**Male
Sex-Related
Organs**

In coping with the problems of impotence and frigidity it is important to understand the sex-related organs and their function.

The female reproduction system is mainly concealed within the body.

The male reproduction system, for the most part, is external. In the male, the visible genital organs are:

---

1. **The Testes (or testicles, gonads)**

**Produce
200 Million
Sperm
Daily**

The testes are two egg-shaped glands. Each is about 2 inches long. They contain a large number of narrow tubules, ducts in which the sperm is formed. It takes about 46 days for a sperm to be produced. On average, 200 million sperm are made every 24 hours. This formation of sperm is a continuous process which goes on sometimes right up to death. Sperm which are not ejaculated degenerate and are absorbed.[1]

Sperm production is controlled by a delicate balance of hormones. These hormones are produced not only by the testicles but also by the pituitary gland and the adrenal cortex. The adrenal cortex contains more than 30 different hormones. They all have the same basic chemical structure and are known as _steroids_. One most people are familiar with is _cortisone._

---

[1]The Rand McNally Atlas of the Body and Mind (New York: Rand McNally and Company in association with Mitchell Beazley Publishers Limited, London) 1976, p. 144.

MALE Reproductive System

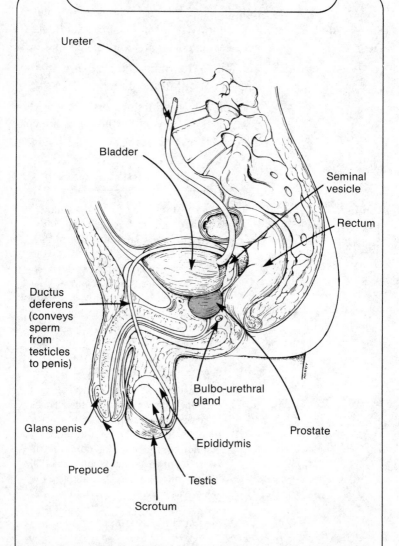

Ureter

Bladder

Seminal vesicle

Rectum

Ductus deferens (conveys sperm from testicles to penis)

Bulbo-urethral gland

Glans penis

Prostate

Prepuce

Epididymis

Testis

Scrotum

**Produce
Male Hormones**

The male hormones _testosterone_ and _androsterone_ are produced by the testicles and are responsible for the development of the male sex characteristics. They also control the sex drive!

The pituitary acts upon special cells within the testicles to stimulate formation of sperm.

The sperm empty into a long twisted tubule. This is called the _epididymis._ This is a single coiled tube which runs down the side of the testis. This journey of the sperm takes about 3 weeks as the sperm go through a maturing stage.

**Area
Of
Vasectomy**

This empties into the _vas deferens._ This slim muscular tube is about 18 inches long and transports the sperm from each testis to the _prostatic urethra._ It is the _vas deferens_ which is severed and tied off in the male sterility operation. This operation is known as a _vasectomy._

The testis are suspended in the bag-like scrotum. This double pouch holds the testicles and parts of the spermatic cord. The scrotum maintains the proper testicular temperature for the formation of mature sperm. Fertile sperm can only be produced if the testes are a degree or two below body heat. This is why they hang outside the abdomen in the scrotum.

**Sign
Of
Sexual
Arousal**

If your scrotum is too cold or you you have stress or sexual excitement, the genital muscles will contract raising your testicles and the scrotum will be pulled into a tight shape against your body. One sign of sexual arousal or a need for sexual fulfilment is that the testicles are raised and the scrotum tightens.

The Prostate

To properly understand the functions of the prostate one should be aware of the bodily interactions that occur during sexual intercourse.

Active in Coitus

Sexual intercourse is termed *coitus*. Coitus means *to go together*.

Sexual intercourse is the insertion of the penis (the male organ) into the vagina (the female organ) during sexual arousal. The insertion of the penis brings about increasing sexual excitement until a climax (*orgasm*) is reached. Orgasm is described as a swelling or fullness and is an overwhelming intense feeling of pleasure. This is centered on the genital area primarily.

Prostate . . . Important In Sexual Relations

During sexual intercourse the heartbeat increases to twice the normal rate. As the climax approaches, an automatic series of muscular contractions occur around the urethra and prostate. This brings about three or four bursts of semen at intervals of about 1 second apart. The prostate exercises such ejaculatory force that the semen can be propelled from a few inches to a few feet. At this point the penis is about 1½ times its normal size but slowly reduces to normal after ejaculation. The amount of ejaculation averages a small teaspoonful.

The man has his orgasm at the point of ejaculation of semen. The woman goes through the same pleasurable stages. However, she takes longer to reach her plateau and can maintain it at a higher level for longer.

Rather than the semen simply flowing into the uterus, the prostate muscles contract and pump the stored fluid along with the sperm and other secretions.

The Explosive Expeller!

The ejaculation has several purposes:

1. Prevents semen from remaining in the urethra and coagulating.

2. Buckshot-type thrust of semen better insures it penetrating the uterus.

3. Climactic ejaculation makes the male somewhat immobile. This prevents him from withdrawing in an attempt to defeat nature's purpose.

The prostate is a vital organ in the male and provides for him sexual gratification as well as the desire. The prostate with its powerful muscular action during intercourse can truly be called the *"male sexual motor."*

3. Cowper's and Littre's Glands

**Secrete
Fluid**

This pair of tubular glands, about the size of a pea, are beneath the bulb of the male urethra. They empty a mucous secretion into it. They correspond to the _Bartholin glands_ in the female. The fluid the Cowper's glands secrete is an alkaline pre-ejaculatory fluid. This neutralizes any acidity left there by urine. This fluid sometimes emerges as drops on the tip of the penis before orgasm.

4. Seminal Vesicles

**Food
Supply
For
Sperm**

At the base of the bladder are two saclike structures. They secrete a thick yellow fluid of milk-sugar semen which acts as a food supply for the sperm on their journey.

5. The Penis

**Dual
Function**

The penis is the male organ for sexual intercourse. It also contains the passage for urine. The penis has distinctive characteristics just as a person's face differs from someone else's. The penis varies in shape, in size, in its tapering and cylindrical shape.

At rest, the penis, it is a soft, limp, tubelike organ some two to four inches in length. It is composed of three columns of erectile tissue: two _corpora cavernosa_ and the _corpus spongiosum_ which contains the urethra.

Sensitive Area

The penis is equipped with both a rich blood supply and an intricate network of sensory nerves. The most highly sensitive area of the penis is centered around the head or _glans penis_.

At birth the glans is covered by an elastic fold of skin. This is called the _prepuce_ or _foreskin_. In 90% of the males in the United States this foreskin is removed surgically by _circumcision_. Removing this skin does not interfere with sexual intercourse.

The main body of the penis is called the _shaft_. Both the main body and the head of the penis are composed of a spongy network of blood vessels and elastic connective tissue.

Ability To Enlarge To Erection

During sexual arousal, the penis becomes erect and stiff and enlarges in size. This is due to the presence of the three columns of tissue in the penis. When sexually aroused, muscular contractions at the base of the penis restrict the return of blood. The penis then becomes engorged with blood and becomes rigid. This is called an _erection_.

While the average penis at rest is about four inches . . . at erection it can range up to 12 inches. The average erection is just over 6 inches.

Size Not Important

Contrary to popular myths, the size of the penis has no bearing on the male's or female's enjoyment of sexual intercourse.[1]

---

[1]Clayton L. Thomas, M.D., M.P.H., Tabor's Cyclopedic Medical Dictionary (Philadelphia: F. A. Davis Company) 1974, p. P-42.

Stimulation Of Clitoris Vital

The most sensitive areas are around the opening to a woman's vagina. The depth of penetration, according to penis size, is less important than how the penis is manipulated to stimulate the clitoris of the female. This stimulation does not depend on penis size.

Continual concern about penis size (or comparing mechanics) can cause an emotional block that could encourage impotency.

Sexual Response Patterns in Younger and Older MEN

	Younger Men	Older Men
Breasts	Nipple erection	Less pronounced
Rectum	Rectal sphincter contractions with ejaculation	Decrease in frequency
Penis	Full erection within 3-5 seconds of stimulation	Erection takes longer Full erection not attained until just prior to ejaculation
	Forceful ejaculation up to 6 inches with explosive contractions during orgasm	Force and ejaculation distance diminish
*Refractory	Brief resting period before next erection and ejaculation	Prolonged resting period of up to 1-3 days before fulfilling another erection and ejaculation

*The refractory period is that time of rest the male requires before he can ejaculate again. This rest period grows longer as the male grows older. Unlike the male, the female does not need a refractory or rest phase after she has achieved orgasm.

1
How The MALE Responds Sexually

A healthy sexually mature male may be aroused to erection by a wide variety of stimuli. Impotence occurs because in one way or another these stimuli are blocked either emotionally or organically (through illness or side effects of drugs).

The most potent stimulus is the direct touching of the husband's genitals by the wife. The sight of one's wife's nude or in a transparent attire at bedtime can also trigger an erection. After several years of seeing one's wife nude, the erection mechanism takes longer to trigger. It is at this point that both husband and wife must not make sexual intercourse a boring routine but a time for renewal of love and affection.

Response to sexual stimulus is a simple reflex. It depends on the presence of sex hormones. If the penis is touched (or any other part of the genitals) this stimulation is relayed through the spinal cord and relayed back to the penis. An erection then occurs. At the same time, this sexual stimulus is conducted along nerve fibers to the brain. In the brain, a sexual sensation arises which links the pleasure-memory of past experiences sexually. This past experience, reflected by the brain coupled with the nerve and chemical stimuli relfected by the spinal cord ... together ... bring about an erection.

Through this interaction, blood vessels open to flood the spongy erectile tissue in the penis. At the same time, the blood is prevented from flowing back because it is trapped through a reflex action. A special valve in the penile veins closes. Thus the once limp penis remains in an erect stage. This is an automatic action.

When a husband finds difficulty in getting or maintaining an erection it is (from a mechanical standpoint) because the *"stop"* valve opens up and allows the erectile blood to flow back through the body. Thus this vascular mechanism is regulated by reflexes of the nervous system which are involuntary. By involuntary, this means you cannot control the action.

In Impotence sometimes the valves to not close at all . . . or they may open too early causing a loss of erection.

A healthy husband can attain and maintain an erection for a long period of time. The longer he can maintain an erection without ejaculating the better he will satisfy his wife's slower sexual response to orgasm.

The most sensitive parts sexually for the male are the penis, the scrotum (testicles) and the rectum.

The initial erection of the penis is called "the excitement phase."

The second stage of sexual arousal is more intense in pleasure and is called "the plateau." This is the stage just before ejaculation in the male (and orgasm or climax) in the female. In this stage, the penis reaches its greatest degree of erection. The penis is firm and the penile shaft is extended to its maximum size. The testicles also are engorged with blood and are about 50% larger.

There may be a color change in the penis with a deepening reddish-purple of the veins. This is similar to the color change in the labia minora of the female.

In the plateau phase, the Cowper's glands in the male release a preliminary clear fluid which trickles down into the urethra. This neutralizes any acidity left there by urine and usually emerges as drops on the tip of the penis just before ejaculation.

The third stage in sexual intercourse is called the ejaculation or orgasmic phase. The orgasm itself has two phases:

1. Emission
   This occurs inside the body a split second before ejaculation. This is done automatically by the nervous system. By a series of involuntary contractions, the sperm and the prostatic fluid are collected from their storage depots in the seminal vessels. They are delivered to the urethra.

2. Ejaculation

As ejaculation approaches, the sphincter muscles of the anus and bladder relax. The heartbeat increases up to $2\frac{1}{2}$ times the normal rate. There can be perspiration and flushing of the skin. The male generally perspires all over his body.

The movements become pulsating and involuntary as the sperm builds up pressure in the urethra preparing for a forceful release.

At ejaculation, there are usually 3 or 4 bursts of semen. These occur about 8/10ths of a second apart. The young male can expel his ejaculation fluid from one to two feet. Generally, the male over 50 has reduced ejaculatory powers and can only expel his fluid 6 to 12 inches.

Men under 30 can ejaculate frequently in one day with little rest in between. However, the greatest pleasure is derived on the first ejaculation. The female orgasm (comparable to ejaculation in the male) gains in intense pleasure in the second and third orgasmic episode. The wife will find these orgasms more sensually pleasurable than the first orgasm.

The fourth and final stage is the resolution stage. In this winding down process, the sex flushes disappear, the blood pressure and heart beat gradually return to normal. The testicles, which were tight prior to ejaculation, relax and return to their lower cool position. In young men the penis can remain erect for another ejaculation. Usually, however, after ejaculation, it first returns to a half erect stage and then to a limp position. Usually in the aging male, the erect penis quickly goes to a limp position within a few seconds.

Penis size or size of a woman's breasts have nothing to do with sexual satisfaction between husband and wife. Popular magazines dealing with erotic sex have done more damage to a wholesome sexual relationship between husband and wife than most any other cause.

24

UNDERSTANDING FEMALE SEXUAL RESPONSE

**Both
Inside and
Outside the Body**

The female sex organs lie in the lower abdomen. The female genitalia are located both inside and outside the body.

External Sex Organs in the Female

The external region consists of 10 structures collectively known as the *vulva*. The word, vulva, in Latin means _covering_. The 10 parts of the vulva are: mons pubis, labia majora, labia minora, clitoris, vestibule, urethral meatus, hymen, Bartholin's glands and Skene's glands, fourchette, and perineum. See page 110 for illustration of female sex organs.

---
1.   Mons Pubis

**Pubic
Hair
Area**

Mons means _mountain_. The _mons pubis_ is the pad or mountain of fat over the pubic bone. The pubic hair, which grows in a upside down pyramid shape, covers the mons pubis area.

2. Labia Majora

**Lips
Of
Vagina**

Labia means *lips*. Thus the *labia majora* are the two thick lips or folds of fatty tissue lying on either side of the vaginal opening. These lips unite above the clitoris. They contain large oil-secreting glands that help maintain lubrication.

3. Labia Minora

**Enclose
Vestibule**

These are two thin lips or folds of skin that enclose the vestibule. They help protect the vagina.

4. Clitoris

**Sensitive
Erectile
Tissue**

This is an organ resembling a miniature penis. It is made of the same erectile tissue and is just as sensitive. It has specialized sensory nerves that are stimulated during sexual intercourse. During coitus it becomes erect and hard. Its erect size can be anywhere from the size of a small button to an inch or even longer.

5. Vestibule

**Almond
Shaped**

The vestibule is an almond-shaped space bordered by the clitoris, the labia minora and the fourchette. The vestibule is usually about 1 inch long and less than 1/2 inch wide.

6. Urethral Meatus

**For
Urine
Discharge**

This is located at the front upper part of the vestibule and is the opening where urine is discharged. The *vaginal meatus* is located in the rear portion of the vestibule. Meatus means *a natural passage or opening*.

7. Hymen (Maidenhead)

**Not
Proof
Of
Virginity**

Hymen means *membrane*. It is an elastic membrane and it partially obstructs the vaginal opening in virgins. Contrary to folklore, the presence or absence of the hymen cannot be used to prove or disprove virginity or history of sexual intercourse.[1]

8. Bartholin and Skene Glands

**The
Lubricating
Fluid**

The Bartholin glands open on both sides of the vaginal meatus. The Skene glands open on both sides of the urethral meatus. It is these glands which produce a slippery lubricating fluid during sexual arousal. This greatly aids the insertion of the penis into the vagina.

9. Fourchette

**The
Fork**

Fourchette means *fork*. It is a tense band of mucous membrane at the rear of the vagina which connects the rear ends of the labia minora.

[1]Ibid., p. H-67.

---

10. Perineum

**Floor
Of
Pelvis**

This is the external surface of the floor or the pelvis. It is the area that extends from the vulva to the anus in the female. It is this area that is sometimes surgically cut during labor to prevent tearing. The surgery is called an *episiotomy.*

INTERNAL SEX ORGANS IN THE FEMALE

Ther are 5 basic <u>internal</u> sex organs in the female genitalia: vagina, cervix, uterus, fallopian tubes and ovaries.

---

1. Vagina

**Opens
Only
At
Intercourse**

Vagina means *sheath.* It is a channel about four or five inches long. At times other than sexual intercourse, the vagina is closed in that its walls lie flat against each other. The vagina connects the uterus and the vestibule of the external genitalia. It also serves as a channel for the penis and the ejaculated sperm to reach the fallopian tubes, for discharge of menstrual fluid and for childbirth. The vagina is usually moist and this increases with sexual excitement.

---

2. Cervix

**Neck
Of
Uterus**

The cervix is the neck of the uterus. It protrudes about 1″ into the vagina. The hormone called <u>progesterone</u> found in birth control pills causes a woman to stop ovulating. This hormone produces a thick cervical mucus that is hostile to sperm and reduces the chance of pregnancy.

---

3. Uterus

**Pear
Shaped
Organ**

The uterus is a pear-shaped organ about 4 inches high and 3 inches wide located low down in the midline of the pelvis. The walls of the uterus are formed by interlaced muscle tissue which surrounds a central chamber.

This internal chamber or cavity is lined with a soft vascular tissue known as *endometrium*. It is this endometrium lining that undergoes menstrual cycle changes and which maintains pregnancy.

---

4. Fallopian Tubes

**Transports
Egg**

The Fallopian tubes were named after Gabriele Falloppio, an Italian who studied anatomy (1523-62). These tubes are about 3" to 5" long and extend up in a curve from the upper corner of the uterus, one on each side, to provide a channel to transport the ripened ovum down into the internal cavity of the uterus.

To accomplish this, each Fallopian tube is lined internally with tiny hairlike projections which help sweep the ovum from the ovaries to the uterus.

---

5. **Ovaries**

**Produce
Hormones**

The ovaries are two almond-shaped organs which are situated behind and below the fallopian tubes. The ovaries produce ova and two primary hormones—*estrogen* and *progesterone*—in addition to small amounts of *androgen*. These hormones, in turn, produce and maintain secondary sex characteristics, prepare the uterus for pregnancy, and stimulate mammary gland development.[1]

---

[1]Diseases (Horsham, Pennsylvania: Intermed Communications, Inc.) 1981, p. 914.

1
How The FEMALE Responds Sexually

As in the male, the female sexual response begins by arousal.

1. <u>The Excitement Phase</u>

   In this intitial phase, the normally tight, dry vagina becomes well-lubricated. The vagina opens up in preparaton to receive the penis *(phallus)*.

   The vaginal blood volume (VBV) increases in this initial excitement stage. Whereas in the male, the penis becomes erect ... in the female, the <u>clitoris</u> balloons into an erect position so the penis can stimulate it. This is sometimes called the *vasocongestive* response.

   A male is easily visually stimulated sexually in seeing a woman's breast or vaginal area. Women, however, are not as sexually stimulated visually in seeing male genitals. More erotic stimuli for women are: slow caressing, gentle kissing, tender touching by her husband of her nipples and clitoris in a teasing fashion.

   While the male's excitement stage is physically evident by his erect penis ... the female is not aware that her vagina is ballooning or that her uterus is rising out of the pelvic cavity to prepare the way for the phallus. She may feel a pelvic congestion at initial sexual arousal and experience a *"wet"* feeling in her vagina. The vagina only expands just enough to accommodate the phallus.

2. <u>The Lubrication Stage</u>

   To prepare for the entry of the phallus, the <u>Bartholin</u> and <u>Skene</u> glands open. It is these glands which produce a slippery lubricating fluid during sexual arousal. This facilitates the insertion of the penis. This is also the *plateau stage*.

Women take longer to reach the <u>plateau stage</u> but they can maintain it at a higher level for longer. In the plateau stage they will begin to show a flushing of the face. The labia lips become swollen and thickened.

3. The Orgasm Stage

   At this stage the labia major and minor lips of the vagina turn in color to a deep red or red-purple hue. This color change is because of the amount of blood that has rushed to the pelvic area ... similar to the blood flooding of the penis to accomplish an erection.

   Women do not experience the same physical release of an ejaculation. But their orgasm is climaxed by a series of involuntary rhythmic contractions. The lower vaginal muscles contract at 8/10ths of a second intervals against the engorged vaginal perimeter. The uterus also contracts and, in a fulfilling orgasm, the wife's hips will move involuntarily in a rhythmic, pulsating, throbbing fashion. These reflex contractions will occur a minimum of 3 to 5 times and a maximum of 10 to 15 times with each individual orgasmic experience. The wife is capable of multiple orgasms. And a husband who fails to understand his wife's sexual makeup is liable to feel threatened.

One of the major causes of frigidity in women is that husbands do not fulfill their wife's needs sexually. In this age of speed, unfortunately they apply the same efficient standards to intercourse.

It becomes a quick communion with no thought given to the wife's personal needs. This is why, in America, less than half the women have orgasms regularly during intercourse. About 10% never experience it!

4. The Resolution Stage

   After orgasm, the uterus moves back into the former pelvic position. The vagina shortens in both width and length. The clitoris returns to its orginal state. It takes some 15 minutes for the deep purple color of the labia lips to return to normal after orgasm.

How The FEMALE Responds Sexually

How do the responses differ in the aging female as opposed to her younger counterpart?

In the <u>Excitement Phase</u> both young and old females experience nipple erection prior to orgasm. While young women also have a vasocongestive increase in breast size ... such response is diminished in those over 50. However most women in the 50-70 age bracket retain nipple erection for hours after orgasm.

The sex flush of women is more apparent in women under 50 and spreads from the breast up to the face. Women over 60 generally do not have this flushing.

The vagina of healthy young women is flexible and rapidly expandable with thick, reddish-purple appearance. In an older woman of 50 to 70 there is often evidence of a lack of proper hormones to maintain good health. If this is the case, the vaginal walls will become thin and there will be a shortening of the vaginal length and width. The vagina may also lose some of its expansive ability.

Whereas in the younger women, vaginal lubrication occurs within 30 seconds of stimulation, those in their 60's and beyond may require up to 5 minutes for vaginal lubrication to occur.

Orgasmic contractions in younger women may be 5 to 10 times ... in older women only 3 to 5 times.

Unless the husband realizes what changes are occurring in his wife, both may lose interest in sex. The husband must be understanding and supportive. And good health in the older years is essential for a healthy sexual response.

25

THE SEARCH FOR SEXUAL JOY

No Magic Pill For Sex

There is no magic pill that one can take to overcome impotence or frigidity. Along with the therapy done at sex clinics . . . a husband or wife can do something on their own to improve their sexuality.

Someone once said that ". . . *your health is your wealth!*"

And many of the sex problems emerge or become heightened because of poor health. America may be the most well fed nation in the world but it stands low from the standpoint of proper nutrition.

Disease Diminishes Erection

Sexual Stamina Fades

We are so accustomed to eating junk foods loaded with salt, highly processed foods and sugared desserts that we lower our stamina and endurance. And, most important, our body becomes host to a multitude of diseases. At first they are hidden diseases manifested only by aches and pains. Then the husband notices he has problems urinating. He cannot maintain an erection.

His doctor tells him he has a prostate condition. The wife notes his apparent lack of interest in sexual intercourse. There is a lack of communication. One can see how easy it is for the husband to become impotent and the wife to become frigid.

Disease Impairs Sexual Arousal

**Fatigue
Reduces
Desire**

Or the wife, because of the tense situation, may become hypertensive (high blood pressure) and take medication. She may complain of headaches and say she is *"too tired"* when her husband wants sex. The husband may also become hypertensive and take drugs. Or he may become diabetic. And he finds himself unable to have an erection.

Both husband and wife thought that the pleasures of sexual intercourse would go on forever. Suddenly the rosy hue of marriage becomes clouded. Discouragement, despondency, doubts enter the marriage relationship. If only one spouse is unresponsive sexually, the other spouse with a strong sex drive may find sexual relief outside the marriage.

**Couple
May
Drift
Apart**

It is easy to see how an uninformed husband and wife who are normally stable in their marriage relationship ... can suddenly drift apart ... because they lack a clinical knowledge of how the male and female functioning all areas of sexual relationships from youth to old age.

SEX IS NOT IN A BOTTLE

Can Decrease Sexual Desire

Too often the initial reaction is to seek an *aphrodisiac.* An aphrodisiac *is any drug or agent which stimulates sexual desire.*

Aphrodisiacs are a myth ... since most drugs do not enhance but rather decrease sexual desire.

Sexual desire is brought about by a complex set of interactions which involve our senses, our emotions, our quality of health, our age, and our hormonal levels. In today's worlds, afloat with pornography, too many center their thoughts on the mechanics of sex and not on the true, wholesome marital relationship.

The Mandrake Plant

Called "Satan's Apple"

The Mandrake plant has been popular since Old Testament days for its alleged abilities to arouse sexual desires. The Arabs called it *"Satan's Apple."* It has a large, brown root, somewhat like a parsnip, running 3 or 4 feet into the ground. It was thought to remove sterility. There is a reference to this belief in Genesis 30:14. It was used as a gland stimulant. In Pliny's days, it was used as an anesthetic for operations. The patient was given a piece of the mandrake root to chew on before undergoing an operation.

In Old Testament days, the Mandrake was thought to be a love potion. Rachel, anxious to bear a child by Jacob, asked Leah for the Mandrakes (Genesis 30:14). It has been called both the "love apple" and "Satan's Apple." In appearance it resembled a tomato.

The Cotton Root
(Gossypium herbaceum)

An Old Remedy

The bark of the Cotton root (2 ounces) was placed in 1 pint of boiling water. A 2 ounce glass of this concoction was taken by women in the Middle East to contract the uterus. This was used both for relief in labor pains and also to generate a sexual arousal.

HORMONES

There are two kinds of hormones produced by the body which act on the genital organs to enhance their size, sensitivity and responsiveness.

1. Androgen, the Male hormone

Sex Hormone

The word, androgen, means to produce. The male hormone, testosterone is a sex hormone which primes the sex centers of the brain. It increases sexual desire in both male and female.

Promotes Growth Of Sex Organs

It promotes the growth of the genitals in the male and the clitoris in the female. Women who have surgical removal of their ovaries and adrenals lose all sexual desire because they are unable to produce the androgen sex hormone, testosterone. Androgen therapy has not been widely used in recent years. However, where impotence is of an emotional origin *(psychogenic impotence)* a combination drug, Afrodex, has been successful in producing an erection and orgasm in 60-90% of patients tested.[1]

Limited Use

Such therapy can only be continued for about two months. Continued use does produce side effects. In the female, these side effects include: weight gain, acne, water retention, clitoral enlargement, oily skin, vaginal itching and menstrual irregularities. In the male, side effects may include: acne, penis enlargement, testicular atrophy, decreased ejaculatory volume, painful erections.

For male and female, side effects may include: dizziness, headache, sleep disorders, fatigue, diarrhea or constipation, change in appetite, and bladder irritability.

---

2. *Estrogen and Progesterone*

Matures Breasts

These hormones aid in the maturing and growth of the female genital organs and the breasts. The estrogen levels diminish after menopause causing the breasts to sag and the vagina to lose its elasticity. Estrogen therapy can unleash other adverse conditions including possibly uterine and breast cancer. The risk is diminished if the therapy only last about 6 months. Some physicians believe that estrogen therapy may actually decrease sexual interest rather than increase it.

[1]Helen Singer Kaplan, M.D., Ph.d., The New Sex Therapy (New York: Times Books) 1974, p. 274.

HERBS AND SEX

Several herbs are recommended by nutritionists as beneficial to the overall well-being. These include:

Ginseng

Normalizes Gland Functions

Ginseng has been considered a remedy for almost all diseases. In China it is used for nervous disorders and a stimulant. Its abilities for sexual arousal have been exaggerated. It does work through the glands and helps in normalizing functions. If taken over a long period of time it can have a beneficial stimulating effect.

Damiana

Acts As Stimulant

Damiana does act on the reproductive organs as a stimulant. It is a small shrub with smooth pale green leaves and is found in Texas, Mexico and South America. It is also a diuretic as well as a tonic.

Saw Palmetto

Aids Male Testicles And Female Breasts

The partially-dried ripe fruit of this herb is used. This palmetto scrub bush grows about 7 feet high and is found on the Atlantic coast from South Carolina to Florida and southern California. It also is a diuretic and a tonic. It is often used for sinus conditions. It is claimed that it increases the nutrition benefits needed for the testicles in the male and breasts in the female. It is considered a tissue builder.

Juniper Berries

Stimulates Sexual Organs

The ripe, carefully dried fruits and leaves are used from the small Juniper shrub. The shrub is common in North America, Europe, North Asia and North Africa. The medicinal actions claimed include: diuretic, ability to eliminate gas (flatulence) aids in kidney and bladder diseases and may stimulate genital organs.

Most health food stores carry herbal capsules which contain a combination of Ginseng, Damiana, Saw Palmetto and Juniper Berries.

Dong Quai *(Angelica Sinensis)*

The Female Sex Herb

Dong Quai root is famous in Chinese medicine for resolving sexual problems of the female. It is a blood builder and nourishes the female glands. It regulates monthly periods and corrects menopausal symptoms including hot flashes and spasms of the vagina. It has been found to bring relief in a number of cases of menopausal rheumatism.[1]

Dong Quai comes in capsuled form. Women generally take two to three capsules daily. Chinese women have found this herb beneficial for cramps, flooding, suppressed periods, fatigue, tension, hot flashes and menopausal discomfort. It also is noted for reviving sexual arousal by restoring proper blood flow to the vaginal area.

[1]Richard Lucas, Secrets of the Chinese Herbalists (New York: Cornerstone Library) 1977, p. 157.

Advice From Royalty

Barbara Cartland, who has written over 300 books in 50 years ... from romantic novels to health books says:

> A man is not competent without vitamin A. Give your husband plenty of it—you'll get it in halibut liver oil—and if you want to have a really super time together, take Banlon tablets as well.[1]

Amaranth For Flooding Menstrual Periods

Aids Menstruation

For profuse menstruation (flooding), Chinese women prepare a tea with the herb, Amaranth (*Amaranthus hypochondriacus* or *Hsien*). The Amaranth is a high protein plant now grown in the United States. Rodale Farms of Emmaus, Pennsylvania have been successful in raising this plant on their experimental farms. Amaranth may become the most important food source for protein in underdeveloped countries. The Chinese women take two ounces of Amaranth and pour one quart of boiling water on it. The brew is covered, allowed to stand until cold. Then it is strained. The tea is reheated to take the chill off. One large cup of the lukewarm tea is taken four or five times a day.

---

[1]Mary Kenny, Birthday Portrait (Surrey England: Here's Health) July, 1981, p. 87.

In July, 1981, Barbara Cartland was 80. Her son-in-law, Lord Spencer, is the father of Lady Diana Spencer who married Prince Charles of England.

Keitafo Banlon tablets are a Chinese tonic containing ginseng, deer's antlers, doe genitals and sea horse.

26

HOW NUTRITION IMPROVES SEXUALITY

**Good Nutrition
Essential
For Sex**

Good nutrition is important for _all_ aspects of sexual life. This include fertility as well as sexual performance.

Many times, the cause for impotence in a male or frigidity in a female is because the individual is suffering from the effects of poor nutrition.

**Avoid
These
Foods**

Many people with sex problems have trouble handling any food with sugar. The individual may not be a diabetic on insulin, yet he may experience the same problems that diabetics experience. If a husband or wife eat many highly processed foods they are off to a bad start sexually. If they include sugar as a part of their diet in such forms as candy, cake, pies, ice cream, cookies, soft drinks . . . they will eventually pay the toll sexually. The evidence will be more observable in the male . . . for he will find himself unable to have or maintain an erection.

There are some vitamins and minerals that are especially helpful in maintaining active sex glands.

Vitamin A

**For
Testicular
Health**

This vitamin helps in the growth and repair of body tissues. If there is a deficiency in Vitamin A in the male, sexual potency is affected. Vitamin A is important for the good health of the testicular tissue. It also aids the mucous membranes of the reproductive organs.

B-Complex Vitamins

**Helps
Prevent
Impotence**

The B-complex vitamins are active in providing the body with energy. There are several vitamins in the B range. They are so interrelated that large doses of simply one or two of them could cause a deficiency in the other B vitamins. All B vitamins should be taken together as a B-complex supplement. The B-complex vitamins are good insurance to prevent impotence.

B_1 (Thiamine)

**Aids
Pituitary
Gland**

This is known as the "morale builder" vitamin because of its beneficial effect on mental attitude. It promotes a healthy nervous system. Indirectly, by way of the pituitary gland, it aids in the functioning of the sex glands.

B_2 (Riboflavin)

**Benefits
Body
Cells**

This vitamin is vital to the breakdown and utilization of carbohydrates, fats and proteins. It aids growth and is important in the metabolism of all the body cells.

1
Foods For Sexual Health

Some foods, because of their high supply of certain vitamins and minerals, are considered important for maintaining good sexual health. These particular vitamins and minerals aid in circulation and supplying nutrients to the sex glands that are essential. Along with this, one should stay off junk foods, highly processed foods, sugared foods and throw away the salt shaker! The diet should contain more raw foods and salads, less meat, more fish (but not shrimp, lobster, oysters, clams or scallops).

High Nutrient Source	Food
Vitamin A	Calves liver, apricots, asparagus, carrots, eggs, sweet potatoes, parsley, green peppers.
B-Complex	Whole grains, wheat germ, calves liver, dried peas and beans, peanuts (unsalted), brewer's yeast,[1] green leafy vegetables. (Remember, the darker in color the vegetable the richer its source of nutrients. Therefore, Romaine lettuce is far more beneficial for you than iceberg lettuce! And cheaper!)
Vitamin C	Citrus fruits such as oranges, grapefruits, lemons and limes; sprouts, green leafy vegetables
Vitamin D	Sunlight, liver, butter, eggs, fish and milk.
Vitamin E	Cold-pressed vegetable oils, all whole raw seeds and nuts, soybeans, wheat germ oil, wheat germ, spinach and brown rice.
Iodine	Citrus fruits, pears, watercress, artichokes, kelp or dulse.
Zinc	Whole-grain products, wheat bran, wheat germ, brewer's yeast, pumpkin seeds, sunflower seeds and eggs.

---

[1]Three teaspoons of brewer's yeast daily will supply you with the necessary B-complex vitamins. You can mix it in with your juice or sprinkle over a cereal or salad. By mixing a tablespoon each of brewer's yeast, wheat germ and blackstrap molasses with fruit juice ... three times a day ... can rejuvenate a sluggish thyroid. Some nutritionists believe this mixture can provide the nutrients to revive one's sex drive making it vibrant and alive again.

Maintains Mineral Balance

B₆ *(Pyridoxine)*

Vitamin B_6 helps maintain the balance of sodium and potassium. This regulates body fluids promoting normal functions of the nervous system.

For Healthy Nerve Tissue

B₁₂ *(Cobalamin)*

This vitamin is necessary for normal metabolism of nerve tissue. It helps iron function better in the body. It is beneficial for mental depression, insomnia, nervous irritability, fatigue and for many illnesses related to middle and old age.

Glandular Stimulant

B₁₅ *(Pangamic Acid)*

This is a water-soluble nutrient that is isolated from rice bran, whole-grain cereals and brewer's yeast. It is believed this vitamin improves the action of Vitamins A and E and provides oxygen to living tissues. It is thought to prevent premature aging. It is also believed to be a stimulant for the glandular and nervous system. Some nutritionists believe it is helpful for those suffering from cardiac problems or diabetes as well. While it is little known in the United States, it is widely used in Russia. In Russia it is also used for treatment of headaches, insomnia, tension, advancing atherosclerosis and other heart ailments.

Vitamin C *(Ascorbic Acid)*

Insurance Against Infection

Vitamin C has many functions. It is essential for healthy blood vessels. It is important also because it aids in the metabolism of two amino acids. It protects against infection and is a good preventive vitamin for those who are prone to cystitis or prostatitis . . . which inflammatory diseases interfere with one's sex life. Vitamin C remains in your body usually only 3 or 4 hours after you take the supplement . . . unless it is a timed or slow release pill.

Vitamin D

Aids Nervous System

This vitamin is the *"sunshine vitamin"* because its primary source is the sun. Vitamin D aids in the absorption of calcium in the intestinal tract and the breakdown and assimilation of phosphorus. Vitamin D is needed to maintain a stable nervous system.

Vitamin E *(Tocopherol)*

Promotes Normal Blood Flow

Vitamin E is often referred to as the *"sex vitamin."* It is an antioxidant . . . that is, it prevents saturated fatty acids and Vitamin A from breaking down and combining with other substances that may be harmful to the body. Vitamin E, through its function, increases stamina and endurance. It helps bring nourishment to the cells, permits a fuller flow of blood through the blood vessels by dilating these vessels. Perhaps in this action, it improves the function of the sexual glands. The open blood vessels of the penis can then swiftly come to erection. And the increased blood congestion in the vaginal area of the woman can increase her pleasurable orgasm.

**Minerals
Essential
For
Sex**

Minerals are often called *trace elements* . . . because they are present in such tiny amounts in your body. There are about 30 minerals and they comprise about 5% of your body weight. They are extremely essential to good health. And good health is essential for a satisfying sex life in marriage! Most people do not realize that vitamins cannot work without the presence of minerals in the body.

**Stimulate
Hormone
Secretion**

Minerals have many functions in the human body. One of the important functions for sexual health is that minerals stimulate the hormonal secretion of glands. This stimulation causes the nervous system to send communicative signals to all parts of your body. This aids in maintaining an erection and also gives a sexual fullness to the vagina.

**Iodine
Fuels
Thyroid**

Iodine is a mineral which is a part of *thyroxine*. Thyroxine is a thyroid hormone. Thyroid hormones are responsible for the sex drive. Although iodine is found in iodized salt, the better sources are citrus fruits, pears, watercress and artichokes.

**Zinc
Helps
Sex Drive**

Zinc is a mineral that has long been recognized as vital to the sex organs. Zinc aids in the general growth and development of the reproductive organs. It also is important for the normal functioning of the prostate gland. Both Zinc and Vitamin E are considered by many nutritionists to be vital in maintaining sexual powers.

1
The MINERAL Approach To Impotence/Frigidity
An Interview with Paul Eck

Dr. Paul Eck has a degree in the field of <u>naprapathy</u>. Naprapathy is a system of therapy which attributes all disease to disorders of the nervous system, ligaments and connective tissue.

He is director of Analytical Research Laboratories in Phoenix, Arizona which specializes in interpreting hair tests. Paul Eck prepares vitamin and mineral programs for many medical doctors and other health practitioners.

Dr. Eck has very definite views on how to correct basic illnesses. They differ quite dramatically from the standard medical approach to disease. In fact, they differ also from many of the usual nutritional approaches to disease, as well!

Dr. Eck believes that much of what is going on today in the field of nutrition is guesswork. Too many people are spending anywhere from $5000 to $15,000 to correct health deficiencies and are no better off physically. The problem, as Eck sees it, is that it is not the products they are taking that are wrong . . . but that the necessary knowledge and application to <u>utilize</u> these various nutrients is missing!

In an interview with Sam and Loren Biser of <u>The Healthview Newsletter</u>, Eck commented:

> It's not the amount of vitamins that you take nor is it the amount of minerals you are taking or anything else . . . the products or the money that you are spending . . . I think a lot of this is pure waste because if it is not being applied in a scientific way there's no way that it's ever going to work![1]

---

[1]Paul Eck, <u>Your Minerals and Your Health</u> (To secure this one hour cassette, send $10 <u>direct</u> to Healthview Newsletter, Box 6670, Charlottesville, Virginia 22906)

Other cassettes by Dr. Paul Eck on various metabolic dysfunctions and philosophy of health are available from Analytical Research Laboratories, Inc., 2338 West Royal Palm Road, Suite F, Phoenix, Arizona 85021.

The MINERAL Approach To Impotence/Frigidity
An Interview with Paul Eck

When Paul Eck first became interest in hair analysis he discovered he had a low zinc level of 9 (the normal zinc level is 20). He also had hypoglycemia, he was nervous and had a tendency towards diabetes. He also knew his anxiety levels were high.

To try and correct his low zinc level he began taking 3 zinc tablets a day. He was surprised to find that he did not get better. In fact, he became worse and experienced extreme fatigue. He decided to go off the zinc and his energy level began to come back to what it was before.

Simply adding zinc to your system can cause other problems. Too much zinc has a tendency to make your copper level low. The normal level for copper in the human body, according to Eck, is 2.5mg./% He states that anyone with a copper level of 1.0 is in a potential cancerous state.

Low copper levels symptoms may show up as: fatigue, anemia, joint pain and depression. Eck believes this can lead to a cancerous condition because:

> ... the copper inside the cell regulates the respiratory oxidation mechanism which prevents you from getting cancer.[1]

Paul Eck also says that if one has a high copper level ... and takes a multiple vitamin/mineral tablet or supplement that has copper in it, their physical problem will become worse. The additional copper, adding to their already high level, will accentuate their illness and the other vitamins and minerals in the daily supplement will be of no value. The indiscriminate taking of vitamins and minerals can be a hit and miss type of therapy. It can be a total waste of money, according to Eck. He believes that up to 90% of the people taking multiple vitamin supplements are damaging their health.

Eck states that copper is the most dangerous of all the required minerals, if you are not aware of what your body requires. Simply to take copper supplements on a guess-basis can be hazardous to your health.

---

[1]Ibid.

Paul Eck also believes that excessive Vitamin C taken over a considerable length of time and in certain "biological types" can cause cancer. He suggests that soils that are high in calcium and magnesium protect against cancer. Any mineral, therefore, that can lower these two minerals (calcium and magnesium) or copper can cause a cancerous condition.

In a recorded interview for The Healthview Newsletter, Eck stated:

> There is no question that a person can take Vitamin C in some cancer cases and derive results.
>
> But, just as zinc lowers copper, which is perhaps the most protective mineral against cancer ... Vitamin C also has a copper lowering effect, and over the years, can cause cancer.[1]

Dr. Paul Eck does not believe it is necessary in the majority of cases to give large doses of Vitamin C. He says that copper makes up a part of an enzyme called ascorbic acid oxidase. An oxidase is a catalyst. It is the copper in this formula that activates the enzyme. If this ascorbic acid oxidase enzyme is missing, Eck believes then that Vitamin C cannot be oxidized to adequate amounts in the body. Therefore, Eck concludes, if this optimal oxidation is not taking place, large amounts of Vitamin C are not only useless but can initiate various disease proccesses.

If your body is not functioning properly, the vitamins will not excrete the excess minerals you may be taking in your daily supplements. Instead they accumulate in the body. If your body is deficient in Vitamin B[6], as an example, you will have a tendency to accumulate copper in the body. This can result in a toxic level of copper in your system.

Dr. Eck does not encourage the taking of multiple vitamins and minerals. He feels this indiscrimate use is detrimental to one's health ... since every individual is biochemically different.

---

[1]Ibid.

Paul Eck is a firm believer in using hair analysis tests. The reason, he states:

> *A hair analysis test is the only method developed that has any validity at all as far as measuring what actually is occurring in the tissues of the body.*
>
> *It has the benefit of being able to give you a metabolic pattern of every metabolic activity that is occurring in your body over a period of time.*[1]

Dr. Eck believes that blood tests, in this context, are frequently invalid because they give you an up-to-the-minute readout. It is not a true reflection of what is happening in the tissues over a period of time. A person taking a high amount of Vitamin C could be releasing from his system large amounts of cholesterol. If a blood test were taken at that time it would show a high cholesterol level. However, what the physician does not realize is that it is not a build-up of cholesterol but, quite the opposite, a beneficial flushing of cholesterol out of the body.

Too many people, Dr. Eck suggests, take maganese when they have a manganese deficiency . . . they take iron when they have an iron deficiency, etc. **This is wrong.** To give iron to raise iron is to lower iron!

Dr. Louis Kervan, in his book, Biological Transmutations makes the following observations:

> For IRON deficiency . . . give Manganese.
> For MANGANESE deficiency . . . give Copper.
> For MAGNESIUM deficiency . . . give Zinc.
> For ZINC deficiency . . . give Magnesium.

---

[1]Ibid.

5
The MINERAL Approach To Impotence/Frigidity
An Interview with Paul Eck

When you go on a correct vitamin/ mineral supplementation, the excess minerals and toxic minerals (such as cadmium, lead, aluminum) will start to unload and flush out of your system. This unloading will cause headaches and numerous other symptoms which will vary with the toxic metal or combination of toxic metals being eliminated, and in some cases make you feel worse. This is a natural occurrence as your body gets rid of these unwanted elements to get you on the road to full recovery.

Dr. Eck believes that mineral imbalances should be corrected mainly by using <u>small</u> potency vitamins and minerals. He says it just takes a very small amount of a mineral to initiate a major physiological process in the body. Any amount over that, he states, will cause exactly the opposite reaction.

Paul Eck believes that mineral therapy is also indirectly hormone therapy. Through the results found in hair analysis he has been able to see people go off hormone therapy, estrogen, even off of thyroxin. He has used manganese and copper to improve their thyroid function where indicated.

Paul Eck is very familiar with Diabetes. His grandmother, his mother was diabetic. He and his brother were pre-diabetic. Dr. Eck states he can determine from a hair analysis, years in advance, whether a person will become a diabetic.

Paul Eck says that 90% of the people who have diabetes have more than enough insulin circulating in their blood. When you have a low calcium to magnesium ratio (such as 3.3 to 1) you have an individual that has diabetes. And if the ratio is high, such as <u>10</u> parts calcium to <u>1</u> part magnesium . . . you are in the diabetic area.[1]

Eck states:

> *One problem in about 10% of the diabetics is the lack of calcium in the pancreas. This condition results in an inability of the Islets of Langerhans to secrete insulin . . .*

---

[1]The calcium to magnesium <u>ratio</u> normally is 6.7 to 1. This means for every 1 part of magnesium in your system, you should have 6.7 parts of calcium.

because when the calcium drops below a certain level you can't even initiate the secretion of the insulin that is manufactured and is being stored in pancreatic Islets of Langerhans tissue.

So what you have to do is, by one means or another, raise the calcium level back up to a close to normal ratio between the magnesium and then you automatically get a secretion of insulin.

This occurs in your insulin-deficiency diabetics ... which only accounts for about 10 or 12% of the cases.

Dr. Eck states that the rest of the problem in diabetes lies either in the transport of the insulin to the cell itself or, when it gets to the cell, there is a lack of a receptor at the cell site on the cell membrane. Those receptors are all minerals! Therefore, Dr. Eck concludes:

If the proper mineral is not available in the body for transport of the insulin to the cell ... it doesn't get there in the first place.

Secondly, even when it gets there, if some receptor is not present, and there are multiple receptors on the cell membrane ... then, of course, the insulin can't even enter the cell and do what it is supposed to do!

We have had such great reports especially in diabetes.

You know the old saying that says "Once you've been on insulin, you're going to stay on it the rest of your life ..." that's the same statement they use for hypothyroidism. They say: "Once you're on thyroid, you're going to be on it forever. Make up your mind to it."

Some individuals have been able to have their insulin requirement reduced or completely eliminated within a few weeks. These, of course, are spectacular cases. There are also insulin-taking diabetics who require a year or two to bring about a complete correction. The individual must be extremely cooperative. Attempts to correct diabetes must be done under the supervision of a doctor.

Dr. Eck says that those taking oral hypoglycemic agents for diabetics are the easiest cases to correct. Correcting those with juvenile diabetes is much more difficult ... unless the individual faithfully stays on the health program.

The MINERAL Approach To Impotence/Frigidity
An Interview with Paul Eck

Dr. Eck believes there are 7 mineral clues as to whether a person is developing cancer. The more of these clues they have the more severe their condition is. Here are the clues:

*1. Calcium/Magnesium ratio of less than 2 parts of calcium to 1 part of magnesium . . . is a cancer indicator.

*2. Calcium/Magnesium ratio of over 14 parts of calcium to 1 part of magnesium . . . is a cancer indicator.

*3. Sodium/Potassium inversion. Normally sodium is 25 in ratio to your potassium, which is 10. This is a 2.5 to 1 sodium to potassium ratio. If the ratio inverts (goes lower than 1.5 to 1) this could be indicative of cancer, kidney disease, hypertension, infections, osteoarthritis, etc.!

*4. Zinc/copper ratio of over 16 parts of zinc to 1 part of copper . . . is a cancer indicator.

*5. Zinc/copper ratio of less than 4 parts of zinc to 1 part of copper . . . is a cancer indicator.

*6. Copper greater than 10 and less than 1.0 irregardless of ratio's . . . is a cancer indicator.

*7. Iron greater than 10 and less than 1.0 . . . is a cancer indicator.

Paul Eck believes that there are important interrelationships between minerals and vitamins. An excess of one mineral can cause an imbalance in another mineral in your body. Such imbalances can lead to illness. Here are some examples:

1. MANGANESE
   Manganese can lower magnesium levels in the body. If your magnesium level is already low, the additional lowering by taking manganese can cause epileptic seizures and other neuro-muscular dysfunctions.

2. CALCIUM
   Whenever you take large amounts of calcium, Eck states you will lose potassium. He says about 80% of the people in the United States suffer from a sluggish thyroid. This causes a high blood cholesterol, lack of incentive, fatigue. Eck says:

---

*These ratios figures are Paul Eck's testing figures. They are not standard ratio figures. What other testing laboratories for hair analysis may consider a normal ratio . . . Eck may consider not in the normal range.

Potassium is necessary for thyroxin, which is a hormone of the thyroid gland.

Therefore, if one takes calcium causing a lowering in potassium he will have a lowering of thryoid function.

Calcium will also drive magnesium out of the body causing a high level of phosphorus to occur and make one prone to dental cavities.

3. Vitamin B$_1$

   Large amounts of Vitamin B$_1$ can over a period of time cause a manganese deficiency. Initially, the taking of Vitamin B$_1$ *(thiamine)* will give you a burst of energy. The excess of this B vitamin may also cause a magnesium deficiency. Both manganese and magnesium are important, Eck says, in blood sugar problems. Because of this manganese/magnesium dificiency, Eck believes, they can develop over 70 different diseases . . . including diabetes.

4. IRON

   Iron supplements can cause a copper deficiency. When too much iron is taken, Eck states, you can cause extremely high blood pressure, migraine headaches, and arthritis. Many arthritics have iron deposits in the joints of the body. Eck also reveals:

   Over 51% of all the cases of heart disease have been found to have iron pigment deposits in the cardiac cells of the heart . . . largely from taking too much iron or an inability to properly metabolize iron.[1]

   To give iron to raise iron is to lower iron. This is true of every mineral. When you have an iron deficiency, you give manganese.

5. ZINC

   Zinc supplements can cause a copper deficiency resulting in a severe anemia. By causing a copper deficiency the following conditions may result—menstrual problems, prostrate disorders, allergies, arthritis and insomnia to name a few.

6. COPPER supplements can over a period of time result in a Vitamin C deficiency. Excessive copper can also cause a Vitamin B-1 and B-6 deficiency.

---

[1] Ibid.

The MINERAL Approach To Impotence/Frigidity
An Interview with Paul Eck

Impotency and frigidity problems are intimately associated with mineral ratio imbalances caused by "stress," diabetes, hypothyroidism, adrenal insufficiency, etc.

The **seven** main indicators, from a hair analysis, of impotence in a male or frigidity in the female are:

1. A 3.3 to 1 or less of calcium to magnesium level indicates that the individual has sexual problems of impotence or frigidity. This inverted ratio is found particularly in diabetics.
2. Sodium/Potassium inversion. The normal ratio is 2.5 of sodium to 1 of potassium. If this is inverted (less than 1.8/1), it is an indicator of sexual problems.
3. Copper. A very high copper level is another indicator.
4. Zinc. Extremely low or high zincs can also indicate sexual dysfunction and be a cause of impotence or frigidity.
5. A Sodium/Magnesium ratio greater than   18/1.
6. A Sodium/Zinc ratio greater than   8/1.
7. A Calcium/Sodium ratio greater than   10/1.

In the problems of obesity (overweight), Dr. Eck breaks down individuals into broad categories such as:

Fast oxidation
Slow oxidation
Mixed oxidation

There are   3   different ways people metabolize their food. Dr. Eck refers to this as *Oxidation.* Oxidation is the use or burning of foods to produce energy on a cellular level. Regarding oxidation, Dr. Eck identifies the categories and suggests:

1. They are so fast
they are breaking down their sugars very rapidly and they have a great increase in heat production as a result. They are the type of people who, when they eat, they perspire a lot. They are *"fast oxidizers."* A *"fast oxidizer"* is a person who has a hyperactive thyroid and hyperactive adrenal glands. They tend to have excessive energy levels due to the fast burning of foods, followed by exhaustion.

2. **They are so <u>slow</u>**
   that they are metabolizing their foods very slowly. They are *"slow oxidizers."* They have a hypoactive thyroid and hypoactive adrenal glands. Slow oxidizer's energy levels are usually low. This can be due to a number of factors such as the body's inability to completely break down the foods consumed when a HCl (Hydrochloric acid) deficiency is present. Low thyroid and adrenal activity also contributes to slow oxidation as well as toxic metal accumulation and dietary habits.

3. **They are <u>mixed</u> oxidizers**
   who may be fast in one glandular area and slow in another. They tend to have energy swings as well as mood swings. This is due to the *"seesaw"* effect from fluctuating into fast and slow oxidation.

Both the fast and slow oxidizers are handling their foods the wrong way.

The Pill Destroys Sex Life Of Women

Dr. Eck believes that the Pill has destroyed the sex life of at least 10 million women.

The Pill creates a false pregnancy. The taking of a birth control pill raises the copper levels in the body. This creates a mineral imbalance which lowers your thyroid function as well as adrenal activity.

When a person has a low thyroid activity (hypothyroid), they don't have anywhere near the sex arousal . . . nor do they have a strong sex desire. They don't have the energy for it! Not only that, but the Pill brings with it menstrual period irregularities and menopausal disorders.

The male with <u>high</u> copper levels also develops a **slow** sexual arousal. Food that are high in copper include Brazil nuts, peanuts, sesame seeds, corn grits, broiled cod, baked flounder, broiled halibut, steamed lobster, pike and perch, ham, liver. <u>Oysters are extremely high in copper</u>. Just 1 cup of oysters (cooked, fried or raw) contains 59 milligrams of copper!

You also take copper into your body by drinking water coming through copper water pipes or cooking out of copper cookware.

Some women wear a copper IUD birth control device. Because the vagina is an acid medium ... that acidity leaches the copper off the coil and it goes into your system. Dr. Eck states that:

> *It is estimated that there is enough copper*
> *eroded from a coil in one year*
> *to actually cause a person*
> *to become schizophrenic.*[1]

In a pregnant woman, the copper keeps building up during pregnancy. The fetus stores a large amount of copper that he gets from his mother's liver. This usually last the child for 12 years.

> *At the end of 12 years ... if the child's copper level*
> *does not go down ... you have females complaining of*
> *acne and adolescent problems, etc.*

If the mother cannot quickly unload the copper excess after pregnancy ... she develops postpartum depression. Some women have become mentally unbalanced after giving birth. Paul Eck believes that copper excesses are the problem. Depending on the mineral imbalances of the individual, Eck uses either minerals or vitamins to unload the copper excesses. The hair analysis determines what supplements are needed.

What Results Can One Expect

Dr. Eck states that those who have a hair analysis and follow through on a personalized supplement program will experience symptomatic changes within two to three weeks. At least one year on supplements is needed to approach normalized mineral levels. Toxic metals and toxic minerals can be flushed out in about 6 months.

They may experience periodic worsening of their general condition depending upon their findings. As an example, if a person has rheumatoid arthritis, many times within the first two weeks there may be a marked reduction in pain. However, if the individual has

---

[1]Schizophrenia is *a major mental disorder typically characterized by a separation between the thought processes and the emotions ... a distortion of reality accompanied by delusions and hallucinations.*

numerous heavy metal accumulation, the removal from tissues and joints of these toxic metals will trigger a temporary flare-up in their condition. This may occur several times throughout the program. Dr. Eck suggests that if this flare-up of symptoms becomes too severe, the individual should reduce or stop taking his supplements for a few days until the symptoms subside.

Permanents, tints, bleaching and coloring of hair does not make any significant changes in hair analysis mineral readings. Some shampoos and hair treatments do affect mineral levels, however.

Selsun Blue may cause an elevation in selenium levels.
Head and Shoulders or Breck may result in elevated zinc.
Grecian Formula or other darkening agents will many
times result in elevated lead levels. Lead acetate is used
in these products to blacken the hair.

Dr. Eck suggests that hair analysis retests should be done three months after the first test to check progress. If the individual is a *"mixed ozidizer"* or *"fast oxidizer,"* a retest is suggested in two months.

Dr. Eck says you cannot treat these people exactly the same as far as anything is concerned. You must take into consideration a broad classification of their oxidation types . . . preparing a program on that premise. You cannot give any one mineral for an obesity problem or any other problem. Hair analysis will determine what minerals are deficient and what minerals are in excess.

Paul Eck is very sold on proper hair analysis. In fact he is so sold on the necessity for hair analysis that he would not suggest any mode of treatment for any condition . . . to a physician . . . until a hair analysis of the patient has been made.

Hair analysis is becoming more and more popular. And there are quite a few hair analysis laboratories throughout the United States. Not all agree with Dr. Paul Eck's approach. In fact, he may be considered a maverick in the field. But his laboratory in Phoenix is kept very busy. It could be a sign that his customers are getting excellent results from his recommendations![1]

---

[1]Dr. Paul Eck, Analytical Research Labs, Inc., 2338 West Royal Palm Road, Suite F, Phoenix, Arizona 85021

27

HOW TO FIND SEXUAL HAPPINESS AGAIN

**A Lasting
Relationship**

Sexual intercourse is a function you should enjoy not only in your younger years but throughout your entire life . . . even in your 70's and 80's!

Male and female were created different . . . purposefully. The sexual organs are present so that husband and wife, through intercourse, can enlarge their family and have children.

**Sex
Strengthens
Ties**

These sexual organs also serve another function . . . that is of a marital communion between husband and wife. This union of their bodies links them physically and emotionally as one. It should strengthen their ties and their love, one for the other.

Unless there is a physical problem, generally, there should be no reason why you should not have a physical love for your mate that culminates in an uplifting, vibrating sexual union at regular intervals.

Here are some suggestions to restore the sexual happiness that you once enjoyed.

Improve Your Health

**Signs
Of
Decline**

Your inability to have an erection or your frigid response to your husband may be due to poor health. You may think you are in good health and not realize that subtly but slowly you are going downhill. You find yourself getting headaches. Sex turns you off. You are too tired. You no longer get repeated orgasms (or any orgasms). Your ejaculation is no longer pulsating. During intercourse, your erection takes longer to achieve. And when you get an erection, it is not hard and solid but semi-rigid. And you feel weak and washed out the next day.

All these are indicators that you are not as healthy as you think you are. In fact, you are sick! And you should start to do something about it . . . not simply for your sexual happiness . . . but for longevity of life!

Follow through on this checklist for victory:

1. Get A Physical Examination

Explain Your Sex Problems

Be frank with your physician. Explain your sexual inabilities. If you can't have an erection . . . tell him. If you find yourself frigid ("turned *off* by sex") . . . tell him. You may wish to have your hair analyzed to correct mineral imbalances in your body. Ask your doctor about this.

2. Correct Your Diet

Ban Junk Foods

Under this guidance, examine your present diet. Get off the junk foods . . . the pretzels, the potato chips, the hamburgers and french fries with those soggy buns. Cut down on your red meat intake (roast beef, steak, etc.). Cut out all pork products including ham, pork chops, sausage.

If your physician approves . . . begin eating a larger proportion of raw foods. Go heavy on salads made with deep green leafy lettuce like Romaine. Add green peppers (seeds as well) and red peppers, string beans, broccoli, all raw!

Get
A
Juicer

Buy a juicer (not a blender) and run apples, pears and the juice of one lemon. Drink a pint of this every morning. Make a full quart and drink the rest of the juice (4 ounces at a time) at regular intervals the rest of the day.[1]

Each morning, add 2 tablespoons of bran to your cereal (or juice). At night, before you go to bed, have another 2 tablespoons of bran with a small amount of cereal (or water).

3. Learn to Communicte With Your Mate

Key
To
Joy

Communication is the key to understanding. How many couples go through life never really communicating with their mate. Oh, yes, they talk with them . . . but they never really reveal their inner emotions . . . their hopes, their fears, things that are causing them tension and trials.

[1]For complete information on juices, you may wish to order How Juices Restore Health Naturally by Salem Kirban. Send $6 (includes postage) to Salem Kirban, Inc., Kent Road, Huntingdon Valley, Pennsylvania 19006. The Getting Back To Nature Diet by Salem Kirban is also $6. If you order both books at the same time, send only $10.

Honest communication is needed in all avenues of life. But it is most lacking when it comes to sexual love.

Be Frank And Honest

When having sexual intercourse, you may like to be tickled. But your mate does not find tickling erotic. Your husband may have worked hard that day . . . didn't take a bath and suddenly at night wants to have sexual intercourse. His body odor turns you off and you tell him you have a headache. Or, you are in your menstrual cycle but you find yourself sexually alive around your menstrual periods. You entice your husband to an erection but as he approaches you, the menstrual odor turns him off and he loses his erection.

You may think the male superior position is the only one that is right. Your wife may want to try the female superior position. Your inbred *"female submissive attitude"* causes you to lose your erection.

Be Sensitive To Needs

You may want your wife to practice fellatio, placing your penis in her mouth for satisfaction. She may agree but finds it distasteful and eventually become frigid. This may be a symbol to her of male dominance and female submission. Or she may want you to practice cunnilingus (licking the vulva). The husband may find this lowers him as master of the house. He may tend towards impotency.

Your wife may wish sexual intercourse at night. You are too tired at night and want it during the day. You may want to have sexual intercourse . . . but your wife puts you off because she has stomach cramps or cystitis or is constipated.

Be Patient

As a wife gets older, she may associate an erect penis with pain. Vaginal lubrication no longer occurs within 30 seconds of foreplay but may take up to 5 minutes and not be as copious. The sudden thrust of an erect penis into her vagina before she is sufficiently lubricated will cause her pain. A lack of communication can bring about misunderstanding. The problem can be overcome by applying a lubricant to the penis before entering, if needed.

Examine Root Causes

You are worried about finances. Prices are going up and your buying power is going down. In spite of this, your husband goes out and buys a new car or a motorcyle or a color TV and you know you can't afford it. Or your wife buys a fur coat.

Your husband does not have a good job. Your wife works and makes more money than you do. You decide to limit your intercourse with her to once a month and practice masturbation.

These are just a few of the hidden reasons why you find yourself impotent with your wife or why the wife may find herself frigid with her husband.

And if you do not honestly communicate with your partner revealing your hidden, secret feelings . . . your desires . . . a wall will be built between you that will destroy your marriage. You may live together and outwardly appear happy. <u>But you are crying inside!</u>

Not One Sided

Naturally, communication cannot be one-sided. Both husband and wife must be mature and understanding realizing they are not identical. Their needs, their personalities, their desires may be different. But it is only by honest communication that the ultimate in sexual happiness can be achieved.

Sexual intercourse is not simply a quick ejaculation and orgasm. The mechanics are not as important as the motivation and the motive.

Don't Let This Happen To You!

I recall a husband and wife who lived across the street from us in the 1950's in Philadelphia. As long as I knew them, they never talked to each other. Yet they lived in the same house but communicated only through a sister who lived with them. I doubt if they ever communicated with each other to their dying day. Yet, if you would ask them what their original disagreement was ... most likely, they would not have been able to recall it! What a shame!

If it makes you happier ... realize that the man you married is not the knight in shining armour you thought he was. Pray for him. Uphold him. Communicate honestly with him.

And husband, if your wife is not the Miss

America you thought you married. Pray for her. Uphold her. Communicate with her.

Happy sexual union can be achieved through honest communication. Why not start this morning . . . or tonight!

4. Avoid Boredom!

Has It Become Dull Routine?

Boredom is the condition of being uninterested. Sometimes, routine can give birth to boredom. Did it ever occur to you in your first experiences of sexual intercourse that a day would come when you would become bored with it? Look back on your most memorable sexual experiences. Now look at you now. What has gone wrong? Don't blame it on age. You can have just as vital, pulsating sex at 80 as you did at 18!

How do you have sexual intercourse? Do you do it as automatically as you open a can of soup? Is it like driving your car . . . you don't really have to think about what you're doing. The actions come automatically.

Boredom can come because of nutritional illness. It can become routine because there is no variety in your approach to sexual intercourse. If you ate scrambled eggs every day at breakfast for years, you soon would become bored with breakfast and your taste buds would lose their sensitivity.

Add Variety

Sexual intercourse is the same. Having sexual intercourse only at night and only a certain day can become boring to some. Or always having sexual intercourse in the male superior position can drift into boredom.

On/Off Technique Selfish

Or if the husband mounts his wife, quickly ejaculates, then brings her to one orgasm by manually massaging her clitoris . . . this routine can become a boring one especially to the wife who is capable of multiple orgasms.

If your husband always takes the initiative for sexual intercourse . . . on occasion, you take the initiative bringing him to an erection.

You can avoid boredom first by honest communication with your mate finding out what avenues of sexual intercourse both would like to explore. Remember, there is more than one way or one time to have sexual intercourse. Boredom can be the death of continued sex. It can also be the death of a marriage!

5. Planned Routine

Avoids Guessing!

Try routine to generate frequency of intercourse.

To some, routine can develop into a boring relationship. Sexual intercourse every Monday and Thursday can become as automatic and as enjoyable as taking out the trash.

While others will thrive under a routine for sexual intercourse.

Too often the wife does not know when her husband wants sexual intercourse. Or she feels she must not start the action going. With each waiting for the other a week or two or more can pass without any satisfactory sexual union.

Particularly if there are problems of impotence and frigidity . . . routine can be beneficial.

Choose Best Days

As an example, decide that you are going to have sexual intercourse every Saturday, Tuesday and Thursday nights (or days). Both partners understand that on those days they will spend time with each other sexually. The wife will prepare and plan for it. The husband will also prepare and plan for it.

The sexual organs needs exercise equally as important as any other part of the body. As someone once said, *"If you don't use it, you'll lose it."* If one's arm were continuously carried in a sling, it would not take too long before that individual lost the ability to use the arm.

For a healthy couple, sexual intercourse takes place about three times a week. For some it is daily, for others mutual satisfaction is gained by only once a week.

Brings Non-Demanding Performance

If there are problems of impotence or frigidity, this routine plan is a non-demanding one. The wife should understand if the husband has difficulty in getting or maintaining an erection. Following the techniques described in this book . . . she can proceed with patience and perseverance. Then, too, the husband knows that a 3-day a week routine has been set aside for sexual intercourse. And his failure to perform one day is not a disaster . . . the other days can bring mutual success. The same reasoning would apply to a wife who is frigid.

Take Time For Love

By this routine both husband and wife can enter into a non-demanding type of sexual intercourse. It need not each time go all the way to ejaculation and orgasm. Caressing, kissing, fondling and hugging may be all that either party needs that night. Or it can be fulfilled to the point where the wife has her orgasms and the husband ejaculates and retains his penis in her vagina all night . . . until naturally separated by sleep.

A routine of sexual intercourse can be a blessing. Misunderstandings, emotional upsets, tensions can fade away and be resolved through this deeper love.

6. Complete Abandonment

Key To Happiness

Complete abandonment is the key to a full sexual joy in marriage.

In today's rushed society, to take more than one minute to do anything (except watch TV) is considered time wasting. We have seminars on how to manage your time and we no longer live by the hour . . but by the minute. We are slaves to our watches . . .

and the second hand. Perhaps we should go back to the sundial days and measure time by morning, afternoon, evening and night.

How often do you find yourself hearing someone talk to you while you are actually thinking of something else!

Not To Service But To Love

With the cares of this world on your shoulders, too often husband and wife participate in sexual intercourse physically, while emotionally or mentally they are wrapped up in their troubles, their trials or their hopes. Their body simply becomes a mechanical vessel to service their mate's sexual desire.

Full Yielding

Abandonment is a French word that had its origin in 1611 A.D. Abandonment means:

> To surrender, to give over.
> To yield oneself without restraint as to emotion.
> An unrestrained freedom that gives way to spontaneity, ardor, unashamed emotion.

In its French origin, abandon comes from the phrase *laisser a bandon* which means *to relinquish to another's control!*

And it is this phrase that most adequately sums up what husband and wife should do when engaged in sexual intercourse. Their mind should be uncluttered and each should relinquish their mind, their emotions, their body . . . to the other's control! That is abandonment . . . in this context.

**Keys
To
Sexual
Happiness**

Good health, good diet, honest communication, banish boredom, regularity in intercourse and above all, complete abandonment while making love . . . these keys can open the door to sexual happiness again in your life!

FOR YOUR <u>LIFE</u> ... KEEP INFORMED!

Now available! A quarterly Total Health Guide Newsletter to keep you up-to-date on the <u>very latest</u> of Medical/Nutritional Data! You owe it to yourself and to your loved ones ... to be fully informed! Now! At last! You can have the <u>most current</u> information on diseases and their treatment ... even before it is available to the general public! The information you receive may help save your life ... or the life of a loved one!

TWO WAYS TO SUBSCRIBE

1. <u>Total Health Guide Newsletter</u>

   Quarterly, for one year we will send you the 8-page Newsletter containing all the latest data on the major diseases. The Newsletter will present an unbiased report on both the Medical and Nutritional discoveries plus reports on their effectiveness and availability.

   One Year: $25

2. **Total Health Guide Newsletter**
   Plus
   PERSONALIZED TYPEWRITTEN UPDATE

   You will receive the quarterly 8-page Newsletter which reports the latest in Medical and Nutritional approaches to disease.

   Plus! You will also receive a TYPEWRITTEN REPORT which you can read in the privacy of your own home. The Report will honestly answer any questions you have on **Impotence/ Frigidity.** *See other side.*

   - You will also receive a <u>RING BINDER</u> to hold the Newsletters and Report. It will also contain a special unit to hold cassettes.

   - Plus you will be sent the <u>cassette</u> ...
     BALANCING YOUR EMOTIONS
     by Dr. Jonas Miller.

     One Year: $50

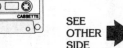

SEE
OTHER
SIDE ➡

SALEM KIRBAN, Inc., Kent Road, Huntingdon Valley, Pennsylvania 19006

- -

YES! I want to keep informed! Send me the Health Information Service I have checked below. My check is enclosed.

☐ 1 Year / $25
Total Health Newsletter

☐ 1 Year / $50 *(Fill in other side)*
Total Health Newsletter
Typewritten Health Report
(Includes Ring Binder/Cassette)

Mr./Mrs./Miss _____ (Please PRINT)

Address _____

City _____ State _____ ZIP _____

SALEM KIRBAN, Inc., Kent Road, Huntingdon Valley, Pennsylvania 19006

REQUEST For Personalized TYPEWRITTEN HEALTH UPDATE

If you are subscribing for Medical/Nutritional Health Information for One Year at $50, you are entitled to a Typewritten Health Update on Impotence and Frigidity.

It is important you understand that we neither diagnose or prescribe. Therefore we **cannot** make personal recommendations to you. Only your physician can do this. What we do provide you is the very latest in both Medical and Nutritional information <u>on the specific problems of Impotence and Frigidity in which you are interested.</u>

Each month we go through hundreds of publications, books and listen to both medical and nutritional seminar cassettes. Your name and the questions you ask on Impotence/Frigidity will be kept in strictest confidence. Your Typewritten Health Update will provide you with medical and nutritional health information as well as emotional and spiritual guidelines. This combination of data should help provide the answers to your Impotence or Frigidity.

QUESTIONS on   ☐ Impotence   ☐ Frigidity

I have been married _____ years   Age:_____

Background: (You may wish to advise if you or your mate have any illness such as diabetes, prostate problems, etc. ... or any other data that may shed some light in answering your questions)

_____

_____

_____

_____

_____

MY QUESTIONS I particularly would like answered: *(Please PRINT)*

1. _____

_____

2. _____

_____

3. _____

_____

4. _____

_____

(If you need more room, attach a letter to this Form)

Mail in this ENTIRE Sheet!
Be sure to fill in Response Form on reverse side
and mail with your check.

NOW! . . . You can make intelligent, life-changing decisions when you know **both approaches** to correcting ailments that plague you or your loved ones!

THE MEDICAL APPROACH
versus
THE NUTRITIONAL APPROACH

NEVER BEFORE . . . in one book . . . has an unbiased comparison been outlined, clearly, simply, showing both the Medical approach versus the Nutritional approach to major diseases!

At last! Sixteen books are now available! Each book defines the disease in words you can understand plus graphic pictures. The symptoms are also outlined.

Each book shows how medical doctors approach the examination of the patient, what tests they conduct, what drugs they recommend (and their side effects), the type of surgery followed and what their prediction is regarding the course of the disease and the probability of recovery (termed, *prognosis*).

In the same book, you will also read the Nutritional approach to the same disease; what natural therapy has been used through the years, what results have been achieved and what the prognosis is using nature's way.

Save by buying several books. Give to loved ones. You may be giving a gift of LIFE! **Each book is $5.**

The Medical Approach versus The Nutritional Approach

ARTHRITIS
by Salem Kirban

(1)

What causes arthritis? How many types of arthritis are there? Does medicine help or hinder? Is chiropractic treatment valid? How will the disease progress if not corrected? What do physicians recommend? What is the nutritional approach to the same problem?

How to recognize the symptoms of arthritis. What diet do many nutritionists feel is beneficial? What foods should I avoid? Answers to these and more!

The Medical Approach versus The Nutritional Approach

CANCER
(including
Breast and Lung)
by Salem Kirban

(2)

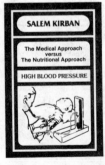

What causes cancer? What do nutritionists believe is the cause of cancer? What are the basic types of cancer? Is surgery the answer? What about chemotherapy? Can drugs cure cancer? What side effects can I expect?

Is a proper nutrition program effective against cancer? What foods should I eat? Should I go on a juice diet?

The Medical Approach versus The Nutritional Approach

HEART DISEASE
by Salem Kirban

(3)

Does a diagnosis of heart trouble mean the end is near? Can I do something about it and live a happy, healthy long life . . . even after a heart attack?

What about drugs and Vitamin E? What is the sensible nutritional approach to the problem? How can I regain a sense of well-being and abundant energy without fear? What foods should I avoid? How can I flush my system clean again?

The Medical Approach versus The Nutritional Approach
HIGH BLOOD
PRESSURE
by Salem Kirban

(4)

Why is high blood pressure dangerous? What are the causes? Is there any way nutritionally to lower my blood pressure? What drugs do medical doctors prescribe? What are the side effects? Do these "miracle" drugs really work?

What is the nutritional approach to high blood pressure? What juices should I drink? What vitamins and minerals are beneficial? Is fasting beneficial? What foods should I eat?

The Medical Approach versus The Nutritional Approach

DIABETES
by Salem Kirban

(5)

What causes diabetes? Must I change my lifestyle? Why do medical doctors prescribe insulin? What is the prognosis for one who is told he has diabetes?

Can a supervised nutrition program minimize the effect of diabetes? Will it provide a normal lifestyle? What foods should you eat? What juices are beneficial? Does the water I drink make a difference? Are vitamins and minerals and herbs worthwhile?

The Medical Approach versus The Nutritional Approach

BOWEL PROBLEMS
by Salem Kirban

(6)

How can I unlock my bowels for better health? How can I achieve that vibrant vitality again and gain that schoolgirl complexion? How can I break the laxative habit? Are drugs the answer?

How can I get rid of hemorrhoids forever? What vitamins and juices are especially beneficial? Are suppositories worthwhile? If so, what type? Can you have daily bowel movements and still be constipated?

The Medical Approach versus The Nutritional Approach

PROSTATE PROBLEMS
by Salem Kirban

(7)

What are the early warning signs of prostate problems? What drugs do medical doctors recommend? What are the side effects? What surgery do they recommend? Is the cure worse than the problem?

Does the nutritional approach offer a more lasting alternative? What diet is recommended? How can you avoid prostate problems in sexual union? Why waiting to correct the problem is dangerous! Do juices and vitamins help?

The Medical Approach versus The Nutritional Approach

ULCERS
by Salem Kirban

(8)

What causes gastric and duodenal ulcers? Are the "miracle" drugs really effective or do they bring with them a host of insidious side effects? What warning signals give you advance notice of an impending ulcer?

What foods are especially helpful? Are juices beneficial? Which ones and how should they be taken? What may happen if you don't change your way of life? What vitamins, minerals are beneficial?

The Medical Approach versus The Nutritional Approach

KIDNEY DISEASE
by Salem Kirban

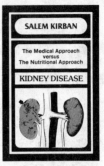

What is the medical approach to kidney disease? What are some of the problems that can develop if the disease is not nipped in the bud? What are the side effects of the drugs prescribed?

Is meat harmful? What type of diet is beneficial? Is a supervised fast recommended? How long? What common, ordinary foods and juices have proven beneficial? What vitamins and minerals help? What about herbs?

The Medical Approach versus The Nutritional Approach

EYESIGHT
by Salem Kirban

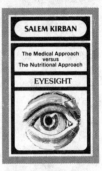

Are glasses the answer to failing eyesight? Is the medical approach to Cataracts the only solution? What do nutritionists recommend?

What eye exercises may prove beneficial for my eyes? Can I throw away my glasses? Is poor eyesight an indication of other growing physical problems? Can diet correct my poor eyesight? What juices may prove beneficial? What combination of vitamins and minerals should I take?

The Medical Approach versus The Nutritional Approach

IMPOTENCE/
FRIGIDITY
by Salem Kirban

Impotence is the incapacity of the male to have sexual union. Frigidity is the incapacity of the female for sexual response. Both of these problems are growing because of today's stressful lifestyle! They lead to other trials!

What is the medical approach to these problems? How successful are they? What is the nutritional approach? What type of diet is recommended? Do juices help? Are herbs beneficial? Much more!

The Medical Approach versus The Nutritional Approach

COLITIS/CROHN'S DISEASE
by Salem Kirban

What causes Colitis? What drugs do doctors recommend? What are the side effects: How successful is surgery? What is the nutritional approach to Colitis? What foods are beneficial? What about juices and vitamins?

What is Crohn's Disease? What are the symptoms? Why does it recur? What is the medical approach to the problem? What is the nutritional approach? Can juices and vitamins correct the cause?

HOW TO BE YOUR AGAIN (13)
by Salem Kirban

How can I restore my energy and eliminate fatigue? How can I develop Reserve Energy as an insurance to good health and a hedge against illness? How can I begin a simple, day by day health program?

How much should I eat and when should I eat? How can I check my own Nutrition Profile daily? How can I feel like 20 at age 60? How can I turn my marriage into a honeymoon again? When should I take vitamins, minerals? What juices are vital for a youthful life?

OBESITY (14)
by Salem Kirban

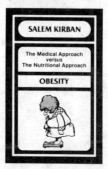

What causes Obesity? Why don't fad diets work? Is being overweight a glandular problem or a dietary problem? Is obesity a liver, pancreas or thyroid problem?

What is the medical approach to treating those who are overweight? What illnesses will obesity encourage? Why does the nutritionist treat your colon? What nutritional approach will take off weight easily and permanently giving you a new lease on life?

HEADACHES (15)
by Salem Kirban

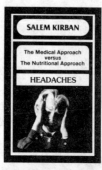

What causes headaches? Can headaches cause depression and hypoglycemia? Are women more prone to have nagging headaches? Must you live with migraine headaches all your life? What is the medical approach to headache problems?

Can a proper nutritional approach rid you of migraine headaches? Do vitamins help? Is fasting beneficial.? What about the pressure point techniques? What 3 herbs promise headache relief? How to tell your migraine *"Goodbye!"*

HYPOGLYCEMIA (16)
by Salem Kirban

Is Hypoglycemia a fact or a fad? Why has this word ... Hypoglycemia ... become the focus of intense controversy? Is it the cause of many unexplained ills? What is the medical approach to this problem?

Anxiety, irritability, exhaustion, lack of sex drive, constant worrying, headaches, indecisiveness, insomnia, crying spells and forgetfulness ... are these all signs of Hypoglycemia? How do nutritionists approach this problem with diet and supplements? Will this approach give you a new life?

ORDER FORM   **SALEM KIRBAN Health Books**

Quantity	Description	Price	Total
	The MEDICAL APPROACH Versus The NUTRITIONAL APPROACH Series		
_____	1 Arthritis	$ 5.00	_____
_____	2 Cancer	5.00	_____
_____	3 Heart Disease	5.00	_____
_____	4 High Blood Pressure	5.00	_____
_____	5 Diabetes	5.00	_____
_____	6 Bowel Problems	5.00	_____
_____	7 Prostate Problems	5.00	_____
_____	8 Ulcers	5.00	_____
_____	9 Kidney Disease	5.00	_____
_____	10 Eyesight	5.00	_____
_____	11 Impotence and Frigidity	5.00	_____
_____	12 Colitis/Crohn's Disease	5.00	_____
_____	13 How To Be Young Again	5.00	_____
_____	14 Obesity	5.00	_____
_____	15 Headaches	5.00	_____
_____	16 Hypoglycemia	5.00	_____
_____	**All 16 Health Books** *(Save $30)*	**$50.00**	_____

Single Book	$5	All 16 Books	$50*
Any 3 Books	$12	(*You save $30)	

Other SALEM KIRBAN HEALTH BOOKS

_____	Unlocking Your Bowels For Better Health	4.95	_____
_____	How Juices Restore Health Naturally	4.95	_____
_____	How To Eat Your Way Back To Vibrant Health	4.95	_____
_____	How To Keep Healthy & Happy By Fasting	4.95	_____
_____	The Getting Back To Nature Diet	4.95	_____

Total for Books _____

*Shipping & Handling _____

Total Enclosed $ _____

(We do NOT invoice. Check must accompany order, please.)

When using Credit Card, show number in space below.

☐ Check enclosed

☐ Master Charge

☐ VISA

When Using MasterCard	Card Expires	Month Year
Also Give Interbank No. (Just above your name on card)		

*POSTAGE & HANDLING Use the easy chart to figure postage, shipping and handling charges. Send correct amount and avoid delay.

TOTAL FOR BOOKS	Up to 5.00	5.01-10.00	10.01-20.00	20.01-35.00	Over 35.00
DELIVERY CHARGE	1.50	2.00	2.50	2.95	NO CHARGE

FOR ADDITIONAL SAVINGS: Orders Over $35.00 Are Now Postage-Free!

SHIP TO _____
Mr./Mrs./Miss   (Please PRINT)

Address _____

City _____ State _____ ZIP _____

SALEM KIRBAN, Inc./Kent Road, Huntingdon Valley, Pennsylvania 19006